Praise for *When Antidepressants Aren't Enough*

"Based on pioneering neuroscience and solid clinical research, Stuart Eisendrath's *When Antidepressants Aren't Enough* provides a wealth of practical exercises that help shift our *relationship* to our thoughts. They can bring about changes in the experience of depression that are immediate and long-lasting. This is a significant contribution to the wise understanding of treatment and recovery from seemingly intractable depression. A gift."

— Linda Graham, MFT, author of *Bouncing Back* and *Resilience*

"This inspiring book makes the best case yet for mindfulness as a treatment of depression. With wisdom and compassion, Dr. Eisendrath shows the reader precisely how nonjudgmental awareness goes to the roots of depression and transforms it for the better. The author has dedicated his career to researching and treating depression. His message is realistic and crystal clear, offering new hope to anyone who suffers from this all-too-common condition."

— Christopher Germer, PhD, lecturer on psychiatry at Harvard Medical School, author of *The Mindful Path to Self-Compassion*, and codeveloper of mindful self-compassion (MSC)

"Living well with depression may sound like an oxymoron, but it is the heart and soul of Professor Stuart Eisendrath's new book, *When Antidepressants Aren't Enough*. With encouragement and compassion, Dr. Eisendrath guides the reader through the process of developing a mindfulness practice that shapes and nurtures a new relationship with the thoughts that fuel depression — a relationship filled with self-acceptance, self-compassion, and peaceful coexistence with our minds."

— Michael A. Tompkins, PhD, ABPP, codirector of the San Francisco Bay Area Center for Cognitive Therapy, assistant clinical professor of psychology at the University of California, Berkeley, and author of *Anxiety and Avoidance: A Universal Treatment for Anxiety, Panic, and Fear*

"The title of this book is very apt. As a faculty member at the UCSF Depression Center, I have seen patients in my clinical and teaching practices respond beautifully to Dr. Eisendrath's mindfulness-based cognitive therapy for depression, even those who did not respond to or could not tolerate antidepressant medication. I have become a staunch believer, and I am so glad that this book will bring Dr. Eisendrath's techniques and approaches to a much larger audience of clinicians and patients alike."

— Owen Wolkowitz, MD, professor of psychiatry and codirector of the UCSF Depression Center, University of California, San Francisco

When Antidepressants Aren't Enough

When Antidepressants Aren't Enough

HARNESSING THE POWER OF MINDFULNESS TO ALLEVIATE DEPRESSION

STUART J. EISENDRATH, MD

FOREWORD BY **ZINDEL SEGAL, PhD**

New World Library
Novato, California

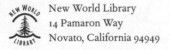

New World Library
14 Pamaron Way
Novato, California 94949

The material in this book is intended for education. It is not meant to take the place of diagnosis and treatment by a qualified medical practitioner or therapist. No expressed or implied guarantee of the effects of the use of the recommendations can be given or liability taken. If you are experiencing serious psychological distress, please seek the advice of a qualified medical professional.

The permission acknowledgments on page 187 are an extension of the copyright page.

Text design by Tona Pearce Myers

Library of Congress Cataloging-in-Publication Data

Names: Eisendrath, Stuart J., date, author.
Title: When antidepressants aren't enough : harnessing the power of mindfulness to
    alleviate depression / Stuart J. Eisendrath,.
Description: Novato, California : New World Library, [2019] | Includes bibliographi-
    cal references and index. | Summary: "A guide to Mindfulness-Based Cognitive
    Therapy as a treatment for major depressive disorder, written by a Professor
    Emeritus of psychiatry at the University of California San Francisco; includes
    meditation and visualization exercises to help readers manage the negative
    thoughts that cause and accompany depression"-- Provided by publisher.
Identifiers: LCCN 2019022185 (print) | LCCN 2019980780 (ebook) |
    ISBN 9781608685974 | ISBN 9781608685981 (ebook)
Subjects: LCSH: Depression, Mental--Treatment. | Mindfulness-based cognitive therapy.
Classification: LCC RC537 .E35 2019 (print) | LCC RC537 (ebook) | DDC
    616.85/27--dc23
LC record available at https://lccn.loc.gov/2019022185
LC ebook record available at https://lccn.loc.gov/2019980780

First printing, October 2019
ISBN 978-1-60868-597-4
Ebook ISBN 978-1-60868-598-1
Printed in Canada on 100% postconsumer-waste recycled paper

New World Library is proud to be a Gold Certified Environmentally
Responsible Publisher. Publisher certification awarded by Green Press
Initiative.

10   9   8   7   6   5   4   3   2   1

This book is dedicated to my wife and family,
whose love and support were invaluable
throughout the writing process.

CONTENTS

Part IV: Lasting Ways to Achieve Happiness

FOREWORD

W e live in interesting times when it comes to the treatment of depression. There is a flurry of interest in finding pharmacological agents that can improve upon the, at times, modest effectiveness of antidepressant medication. On the one hand, increased consideration is being given to repurposing drugs not ordinarily used for treating mental-health conditions and studying their impact on depression. The recent approval of ketamine,[1] a general anesthetic, for treatment-resistant depression is but one example. On the other hand, there is a growing willingness in some sectors to use microdosing of psychoactive drugs such as LSD[2] to achieve mood stability and increase hedonic tone.

What both these trends suggest, and what is borne out by longitudinal studies of the course of depressive disorders, is that treatment of this condition has to account for the acute symptomatology, residual symptoms that persist following care, and the risk of episode return. This is what patients are looking for, this is what providers are tasked with, and this is why Stuart Eisendrath's book could not have come at a better time.

Stuart Eisendrath has worked at the frontier of depression care for most of his distinguished career and has seen firsthand the merits and limitations of the myriad of approaches used to treat depression. The particular wisdom conveyed in these pages reflects the view that, for a large majority of patients, effective treatment of depression is not likely to be achieved via a single modality. Rather, effective care will involve sequencing interventions to enable patients to harness the benefits of multiple inputs.

One method with a strong evidence base for allowing patients to address residual symptoms following acute treatment or prevent relapse following recovery is mindfulness-based cognitive therapy (MBCT). Mindfulness-based cognitive therapy is ideally suited for use in a sequenced manner following either pharmacological or psychotherapeutic treatment of depression, either as an adjunctive form of care, adding to what is already in place, or as the next step once initial treatment has ended.

Stuart was an early adopter of MBCT and, just as Mark Williams, John Teasdale, and I did, stepped outside the confines of his academic discipline to acquire the particular skill set that provides the grounding for effective teaching of MBCT, namely, developing a personal mindfulness practice, becoming familiar with mindful movement, and mastering inquiry into the unfolding mindfulness process. For many of us who were familiar with the tenets of cognitive behavioral therapy prior to MBCT, Stuart included, this sometimes meant responding to group members from the perspective of a mindfulness instructor rather than as a psychotherapist. Stuart's groundbreaking work at the University of California at San Francisco allowed MBCT to be offered as part of routine depression care and carried forward into a number of research studies examining both the clinical efficacy and neural correlates of MBCT.

This easily accessible and carefully crafted book provides readers with a clear-sighted distillation of the clinical wisdom behind MBCT and its particular capacity to address the mind states that often fuel and perpetuate depression. Two helpful conceptual views capture the essence of the approach and allow readers to move into a more fine-grained analysis of the ways these principles can be pragmatically applied on a daily basis. The emphasis from the start is on learning how to develop a "different relationship" to depressive phenomena, rather than expecting that MBCT will lead to their elimination. This is not preached at readers, but rather is illustrated throughout the book by examples of what this "different relationship" looks like, how it may differ from older patterns of avoidance or numbing, and how small moments of willingness and allowing can provide an embodied experience of this relationship. The second overarching principle is "observing your thoughts as thoughts and not facts," and once again readers are provided with clinical vignettes, poetic metaphors, and self-guided exercises to encourage an embodied understanding of what this actually means.

When readers are introduced to the formal and informal mindfulness practices that are featured throughout the book, they will recognize these two elements as core parts of the practice. But my sense is also that, having read the book, they will be better prepared to incorporate them into their lives. In fact, the last chapter of the book makes this point. It specifically establishes the link between keeping one's practice alive and living well with depression. This final note beautifully captures the intentions behind MBCT — supporting people in making wise and intentional choices for self-care in a practice in which mindfulness meditation features less as a form of therapy and more as an act of love and affirmation. This book adds its potent voice to support this healing message.

— Zindel Segal, PhD, coauthor of
The Mindful Way through Depression

INTRODUCTION

When Antidepressants
Aren't Enough

I f you are suffering from depression or have suffered from it in the past, I want you to know that you share a very common human experience. The World Health Organization estimates that at any one point in time there are over one hundred million people worldwide suffering from depression.[1]

This book may not be your first foray into treating your depression. Or perhaps you haven't sought help, because the depression has kept you pessimistic about the possibility of relief. Although a variety of treatments are available for depression, the most common one is antidepressant medication. In fact, over one-sixth of Americans take a psychiatric medication, usually an anti-depressant.[2] Perhaps you are currently taking a medication, but it is not working adequately and you still feel very low.

Regardless of whether this is your first foray or your tenth or whether you have tried or are currently taking antidepressant medication, you have come to the right place. This book presents a new view of depression and how to approach it. I know from both my clinical and personal experience that the techniques provided here can be very helpful.

This book is particularly for you if you've tried treatment

with antidepressants and have failed to achieve full recovery. Such residual symptoms tend to be the rule for depression, not the exception. The techniques found here can be combined with medication or used alone. As with any intervention for depression, if you notice a worsening of symptoms as you practice the techniques, you should pause and speak with a mental-health specialist, but in my experience this is a very uncommon result. Feeling suicidal either before or during your practicing would be another reason to speak with a mental-health specialist or your primary-care physician.

For the past twenty years, I have been on the front lines, as both a researcher and clinician, in the use of mindfulness-based cognitive therapy (MBCT) for the treatment of depression. I founded the University of California San Francisco Medical Center's Depression Center and was its director for many years. My own research and the work of many others have shown that MBCT brings about significant improvements even for people experiencing some of the most difficult forms of depression. MBCT blends mindfulness meditation with some key concepts from cognitive therapy, namely, that we don't need to dig around in our childhood to find the roots of our distress; we can instead choose to change our *relationship* to it.

Many treatments for depression try to *suppress* symptoms, which is often quite difficult to achieve. For example, some traditional cognitive-therapy techniques focus on replacing negative thoughts with more positive ones. This book's approach is quite different: it aims at changing your relationship to depression without focusing on a decrease of its symptoms.

This means recognizing the full spectrum of depressive symptoms and choosing to accept them. Paradoxically, acceptance makes it possible to diminish their impact. Resistance to the symptoms often worsens depression. In other words, we get more depressed about being depressed.

Acceptance is not the same as resignation. Resignation leads to a life of continued suffering. Acceptance, however, opens the door to change. The famous psychiatrist Carl Rogers said, "The curious paradox is that, when I accept myself just as I am, then I can change." Many of you are familiar with alcoholics who did not start dealing with their problem until they accepted it. Acceptance is not submission, but rather a recognition of the facts that are present and then deciding what you're going to do about the situation.

With depression the problem may be more subtle. For example, many people resist the idea that they have a condition in which relapsing is very likely. Rather than recognizing that likelihood and developing an action plan for when symptoms return, they are caught off guard and view each relapse as a personal failure or catastrophe.

Can you imagine a diabetic who is surprised each time she has an exacerbation of her condition? Of course not. That would be denial of the nature of the illness. It is my belief that the same is true for mood disorders. They might never be cured per se, but choosing to recognize that you have a disorder puts you in a position to respond skillfully to it — and to experience the true joys life has to offer.

> Can you imagine a diabetic who is surprised each time she has an exacerbation of her condition? Of course not.

Resisting the experience of being depressed with your entire being often does little other than increase your distress. People may say, "It's terrible I have depression," or "This means I am a weak person," or "I will never recover from this." All of these statements can be considered aversions to accepting the pain of depression. These negative self-statements amplify the impact of the depressive state, which is already bad enough on its own. Of course, acceptance of the pain of depression does not eliminate that pain. What it does is decrease the resistance, and that in itself decreases suffering and allows for a skillful response. We will discuss these issues in greater depth throughout the book.

My aim is to help you prevent a depressive episode or treat a current one that may not have responded adequately to antidepressant treatment or other interventions. I will help you *change your relationship* to depression, so that you can live a more satisfying and happy life. You will learn a number of brief, easy-to-apply meditations that you can start using right away even if you have never meditated before. The MBCT meditations will help build the mindfulness skills that will allow you to change your relationship to depression. I will explain what mindfulness is — in brief, it is an intentional awareness of the present moment without any judgment or criticism of that moment — and how it can help you change your relationship to depression. Although mindfulness meditation was developed twenty-five hundred years ago as a Buddhist practice, in recent years secular applications such as MBCT have broadened its applications and clinical utility.[3] As we will see, mindfulness practices can be extremely effective in lifting you from depression.

How I Became Involved in the Use of MBCT for Depression

Finding effective treatments for depression has been a longstanding passion of mine for several reasons. In addition to founding and then directing the UCSF Depression Center for many years, I was also one of the founding directors of the National Network of Depression Centers, which is tasked with developing effective evidenced-based treatments for depression around the country. The UCSF Depression Center was responsible for implementing treatment plans for thousands of patients during my tenure. Often these patients were referred because they had not responded to the initial antidepressant treatment given by their primary-care physician.

When I initially became familiar with mindfulness-based cognitive therapy, it was being used only to prevent relapse in those considered "fully recovered" from depression. When I attempted to introduce MBCT into our system, I found that there were few patients who had actually fully recovered. My colleague Maura McLane and I then began to modify the original therapy, so that it would be appropriate for individuals who had not necessarily fully recovered and were seeking tools they could use on their own without relying on ongoing sessions with a therapist.

We blended some teaching points from acceptance and commitment therapy (ACT)[4] that share similar features with MBCT into our intervention, as you will see in later chapters. We also modified the original MBCT that was developed to prevent depression relapse in individuals who had fully recovered from a depressive episode. We modified MBCT to make it suitable for individuals who were currently suffering depression. We found that often people were seeking an intervention that might be an alternative to further medication trials. Our modified form of MBCT could provide a skill set that would empower them to cope with their illness.

Another factor driving my interest in mindfulness-based techniques was my own personal experience with depression. For me, antidepressant treatment was helpful occasionally, but at other points much less so. Early in my career, I also entered into psychoanalysis, a popular form of treatment then. While I was suffering with depression, I experienced a great number of guilty thoughts. I thought I was to blame for many things, including problems that in reality had nothing to do with me.

My psychoanalyst suggested that I must have either committed or wished to commit some childhood crime as an explanation for my guilty feelings and thoughts. I spent quite a bit of couch time exploring various possible crimes to explain my guilt. The psychoanalyst accepted the guilty thoughts and feelings as if they were actual evidence of a past real or fantasized crime. This is a common myth that I tended to believe as well. My explorations were an interesting exercise, but of little practical value in helping me deal with depression.

After leaving psychoanalysis, I began to think more about depression and the phenomena associated with it. In particular, I realized that guilt, often termed *pathological guilt* because it is felt inappropriately, is a symptom of depression. Once I learned about mindfulness meditation, which is a form of meditation aimed at giving us the ability to see ourselves from an observer's perspective, to let go of judgment and self-criticism, and to see what truly *is*, in this moment, I began to be able to watch the rise of guilt-laden thoughts within my own consciousness. I found that if I did not attach significance to such thoughts but just observed them, they faded out of awareness.

Mindfulness allowed me to respond more appropriately to the thoughts rather than reacting to them as if they were true. The guilty thoughts were just thoughts — not evidence of some wrongdoing. In fact, they were a common manifestation of depressive illness. The analyst's approach was akin to misdiagnosing my thoughts as facts.

This understanding caused a significant shift in my attitude. It was not that the guilty thoughts stopped completely, but their meaning and impact changed dramatically. As we will uncover later in this book, thoughts, even the ones we may believe most strongly, are merely passing mental events and not facts to be taken literally.

Thoughts, even the ones we may believe most strongly, are merely passing mental events and not facts to be taken literally.

My experience with depression led me to search for something to reduce the stress in my life. I had heard of a mindfulness-based stress reduction course. The course taught mindfulness in an eight-week program. I enrolled in a class and found it so helpful that I took it a second time. It not only helped reduce my stress levels; it offered me a way to begin disengaging from my thoughts and feelings. I became a daily practitioner of mindfulness meditation.

When mindfulness-based cognitive therapy (MBCT) was developed in 2002,[5] I was soon attracted to it as a way to blend my personal experience with a more formalized therapeutic approach. This in turn led me to introduce this modality at our depression center.

Depression is associated with a cluster of symptoms including lowered mood, feelings of guilt and worthlessness, alterations in sleep and appetite, loss of pleasure, poor concentration, decrease in energy, and sometimes suicidal thoughts. It is associated with self-critical ruminations. This kind of thinking is an attempt to solve an insoluble problem, such as reversing something negative that happened in the past. Ruminative thinking is an important driver of depression.

If you are depressed, a negative event tends to have an even more powerful impact on you. You see this event more negatively than it is in reality. This tends to stimulate depressive feelings, which in turn lead to more negative depressive thoughts. This lays the groundwork for a depressive episode. In fact, the more depressive episodes a person has, the more likely it is that this cycle is in fact taking place. Fortunately, MBCT can interrupt this cycle.

Studies have shown that MBCT can decrease depression relapse rates and can be just as powerful as medications in doing so.[6] MBCT helps you see depressive thoughts as just thoughts and not facts, so their impact on producing further changes in mood is diminished.

MBCT also helps prevent depressive relapses by helping diminish experiential avoidance. What does this mean? When depression occurs, it is natural to want to avoid it. Who wants it? Unfortunately, attempts to avoid it, like distraction or substance use, tend to work only in the short run and actually cause increased depression in the long run. MBCT advocates acceptance, not resignation or giving up, which actually helps reduce suffering.

What does acceptance look like? It involves noticing where in the body you feel the depressed feelings. Is there tension in the neck or chest? Is there headache pain in the temples? Are there other changes in the body? When you notice these, you can begin the process of acceptance. Then you can breathe into the body part, saying, "It's okay," and allow the sensation to be present.

MBCT also helps promote acceptance of depression by helping you take a decentered view of it. This means you view yourself suffering from depression as if you were viewing someone else suffering. You can see that suffering is occurring and be sympathetic and compassionate, but it's with some distance and without the criticism so common in depression. As we'll see later, the reason this works is that acceptance techniques are associated with activation of the left dorsolateral prefrontal cortex. This activation is associated with normalization of mood.

We began researching the modified MBCT's efficacy soon after we introduced it at the UCSF Depression Center. I will describe this National Institutes of Health–sponsored research in more detail, but for now let me say that we found modified MBCT to be powerful in an eight-week program and to continue to have effects even as far out as five years.[7]

I am confident that what I am presenting here can be of significant value to you. In fact, it has the potential to radically change your life. Again, this does not mean eradicating depression, but rather changing your relationship to it. It no longer has to be the driving force in your life as you determine your values and pursue your goals.

How to Use This Book

This book can be used as a guide to developing a mindfulness practice. As you read, you will find recommendations for specific meditations entitled "Try This." Many of the meditations can be carried out by simply reading the text. Some, however, may be better carried out by listening to them, and all can be found on my website, www.stuarteisendrath.com, for easy download or streaming.

As you try the different meditations, you will probably find some that will become your favorites and others less so. This variation is completely normal. The goal of the book is to help you develop your personal practice — what works best for you. In order to fully explore the different meditations, I suggest you give each one at least a few tries before moving on to the next. I also suggest that you try to carry out one meditation each day. You can read the book at any rate you choose, but if you carry out the practices over an eight-week period, you will approximate the modified MBCT course we used in our research.

I hope that this book will offer you the same kind of benefit that I and so many of my clients have derived from a mindfulness-based approach to treating depression.

THE NATURE OF
THE DEPRESSION BEAST

Whether you call depression a demon, madness, or a season in hell, it is without doubt one of the most painful human conditions. It is also widespread, and younger and younger people are experiencing its onset. Instead of starting in a person's late twenties or thirties, as it once did, it now typically comes on in a person's late teens or early twenties. It also affects people of all social classes and situations. People as diverse as Abraham Lincoln, Winston Churchill, Ernest Hemingway, Brooke Shields, and Gwyneth Paltrow have suffered from depression.

Mahatma Gandhi described his depression as "a dryness of the heart" that made him want to "run away from the world."[1] Vincent van Gogh described his experience in his diary: "I cannot possibly describe what the thing I have is like; there are terrible fits of anxiety — without any apparent cause — or then again a feeling of emptiness and fatigue in the mind. I consider the whole rather as a simple accident, no doubt a large part of it is my fault, and from time to time I have fits of melancholy, atrocious remorse."[2]

If you have suffered from depression or are suffering right now, you know the sadness, the lack of joy, and the paralysis it can bring. It often impairs cognitive function, so that thinking and even the simplest decisions are difficult. The past looks terrible, the future promises disaster, and you may feel as if you are not worth much at all. Your sleep and appetite may be affected — either increased or decreased. You may be overcome with thoughts of death and suicide along with the feeling of being helpless to do anything about your condition. You may also feel hopeless, believing that no one else can help you. Here's what I want you to know right now: *These thoughts are just that; they are thoughts. They are not facts.* And I'm going to show you how to change your relationship to these thoughts, so they stop having such a firm grip on your life.

There are various theories about depression and what causes it. Currently, our understanding is that both genetic predispositions and environmental stressors play significant roles. There is some evidence, for instance, that genetic predispositions affect how we handle stress.

From an evolutionary standpoint, it has often been thought that depression has a potential adaptive function. For example, in studies of pigtail and bonnet macaque monkeys, when infants were separated from their mother, the infants adopted what appeared to be a depressive state. They would lie on the floor, curl up, and socially withdraw. After a short cry out to the mother, if the mother did not return, this depressive state persisted. So, in this sense, the depressive state was thought to act as a means of conserving energy.

Moreover, it was postulated that the infant monkeys would try to avoid such an apparently unpleasant state by staying close to their mother whenever possible. Thus, the attempt to prevent depressive states from occurring resulted in the enhancement of the drive for attachment of the infant to the mother. In this sense, avoidance of depression served as an adaptive survival value for the infants, keeping them safely attached and under the protective purview of their mothers.[3]

The evolutionary hypothesis for depression is one of many that we consider today. Another causative factor is thought to be stress. The pace of everyday life has increased; coping with modern time pressures and information input can be challenging. An additional form of stress relates to our society's social fabric. As we've become a more mobile society, many of the established social supports, such as having family nearby, have dropped away. When these stresses are experienced along with traditional factors such as grief and trauma, the results are compounded. Biological factors such as genetics, neural transmitters, and brain circuitry also play key roles.

Our understanding of depression has been deepened in recent years by the investigation of brain functioning using moment-to-moment scanning such as positron emission tomography (PET) and functional magnetic resonance imaging (fMRI).[4] These techniques have revealed alterations of brain circuitry in people with depression and suggested that recovery may be associated with restoring more normal patterns of brain activation. These investigations have helped to shed light about what areas of the brain are most involved in depression and how interventions can be targeted toward those areas. For example, antidepressants and electrical or magnetic brain stimulation may be used to normalize altered patterns of activation. As we will discuss later, mindfulness interventions such as MBCT may have powerful brain impacts of their own.

Depression Is Not a One-Time Event

One thing we know for sure: depression tends to be chronic and recurrent. It is not a disease like pneumonia that happens once and then (usually) never happens again. It is more like asthma;

you can expect to have episodes intermittently throughout your life. You must understand this vital point, so that when depressive episodes hit, you see them for what they are: recurrences of your illness and not personal weakness or moral failure.

With depression, the chance of having a recurrence increases with the number of episodes you've had. For example, with one episode, there is up to a 30 percent chance of recurrence within ten years. With three episodes, the likelihood of having a recurrence within that same time frame is 90 percent. The ability to "recover" from a depression does offer the best chance of preventing further episodes, and people can go for substantial periods of time without recurrence, but depression is not typically cured, and even in remission people may have lingering symptoms. Because of the likelihood of recurrence, I want you to have and know how to use the tools that MBCT can provide both to keep depression at bay and to deal with depressive symptoms when they arrive.

When depressive episodes hit, you must see them for what they are: recurrences of your illness and not personal weakness or moral failure.

But let's be clear. Although remission is often portrayed in rather glowing terms in pharmaceutical advertisements, it is not easily achieved. In fact, failure to achieve full remission shows the tenacity of your illness. It is typical, and it is not a personal weakness. Of course, not achieving remission occurs with other illnesses as well. Not many people achieve remission with medical conditions such as diabetes, hypertension, or chronic lung disease. Like depression, these illnesses tend to be chronic. That is why our modified MBCT approach is aimed at the illness rather than only a single episode.

The largest and longest study of depression ever completed at the National Institute of Mental Health, the Sequenced

Treatment Alternatives to Relieve Depression (STAR*D) study, investigated different approaches to depression treatment.[5] In the study, the initial treatment consisted of administering a selective serotonin reuptake inhibitor (SSRI), the most commonly utilized class of antidepressant, for twelve weeks. The remission rate was 28 percent after this first treatment. If individuals did not achieve remission after that one antidepressant trial, they were given another antidepressant trial, an augmenting agent, or traditional cognitive therapy.

After this second step, the cumulative remission rate was approximately 50 percent. This meant, however, that half of the people had not achieved remission despite twenty-four weeks of monitored treatment in the study. After two additional twelve-week interventions (making a total of forty-eight weeks of treatment), only 43 percent of individuals were in remission, including participants who achieved remission but then suffered a relapse. These results illustrate the challenges facing those with depression.

This book is not written to denigrate antidepressants or traditional therapy. They can be lifesaving at times. But they have their limits, a point that applies to other forms of psychotherapy as well.

For example, for a number of years I taught cognitive therapy groups for individuals with chronic depression. In traditional cognitive therapy, negative thoughts (cognitions) are considered to be an important driver of depressed mood, and individuals are taught to challenge them. In this model when individuals express a negative belief or thought, they are encouraged to develop a more balanced or alternative thought. But this may be particularly difficult when individuals have suffered chronic depression lasting two or more years. Some people simply find it too difficult to counter their negative thoughts and beliefs.

If you have suffered depression for some time, I'm sure you

get it. It is likely that you believe you have strong evidence to support your negative thoughts and beliefs due to many years of experience in interpreting yourself and your environment in a negative way. If you have been depressed for years (in our research, the Practicing Alternatives to Heal from Depression study, PATH-D, which is described in detail in Appendix A, participants averaged seven years of depression for their current episode), I'm sure you have accumulated quite a bit of evidence to support your pessimistic thinking. That's in large part because depression has a tendency to put a negative filter on memory and experiences. For example, if we have been rejected in one social situation, we typically expect further rejections, often blaming ourselves for the rejection. It's really hard to counter that with alternative thoughts.

Enter Mindfulness

The unique form of meditation that is mindfulness meditation offers a different approach. Other types, such as Transcendental Meditation and some forms of Judeo-Christian meditation, are concentrative; they focus on a particular phrase or word. Mindfulness meditation differs in that it is intentionally fixed on a focus the meditator chooses. For example, it may be focused on the breath moving in and out of the nostrils, bodily sensations, thoughts, or feelings. It allows meditators to observe themselves participating in experiences in real time, as those experiences are occurring. Mindfulness meditation is sometimes referred to as *insight meditation*, as it allows meditators to see things as they really are.

Mindfulness meditation traces its roots to Buddhist practices of twenty-five hundred years ago. The Buddha is said to have utilized his own mindfulness practices, including sitting and walking meditations. Over the centuries, mindfulness meditation has spread beyond its Asian beginnings. Modern mindfulness meditation can be traced to the Theravada tradition of Buddhism in the eighteenth century, where the meditative component of Buddhism was emphasized. In the mid-twentieth century Mahasi Sayadaw began to change the focus of meditation to center on a present-moment awareness of the sensations in the body, which is typically done through an exercise called the body scan.[6] The mindfulness practice was further secularized and given a broader audience when Jon Kabat-Zinn introduced his Mindfulness-Based Stress Reduction (MBSR) program at the University of Massachusetts at Worcester in 1979, which was built around the principles he later elucidated in his classic book *Full Catastrophe Living*.[7]

The MBSR program offered a way for a large number of people to explore mindfulness unhindered by religious or philosophical concepts. The program offered an eight-week course that facilitated empirical research regarding its efficacy. The program proved beneficial for a wide variety of conditions, such as chronic pain, heart disease, cancer, psoriasis, anxiety, and generalized stress.[8] As a condensation of mindfulness practices into a discrete program, MBSR appealed to a wide-ranging audience. Importantly, it offered a platform that could be built upon for specific applications. In fact, it was the forerunner of the MBCT program as well as other mindfulness-based interventions. MBCT bears many similarities to MBSR, such as utilizing comparable meditation practices. MBCT differs by being more focused on depression and anxiety in contrast to MBSR's broader scope.

Mindfulness is focused on the present moment. You incline your mind to focus on something that is occurring right now. Often you may begin with focusing on the breath moving in and out, perhaps at the nostrils but at other times in the chest or abdomen. The breath is a neutral object of attention for most people and is always present during life. Breathing can be experienced with little thought or effort. It is naturally tied to the present moment

— typically you don't spend much time focusing on your last breath or the upcoming one.

Many meditations start with the breath and then shift to another object of attention. For example, with the body scan, you typically start with the breath and then investigate the senses in areas of the body, starting in one limb and moving progressively throughout the body. But you do not need to begin with the breath in every meditation.

Mindfulness meditation is like a spotlight that you can choose to direct anywhere you want. It puts a bright light on the object of attention. You can aim it at physical sensations, but also at thoughts that are emerging or at feelings that are present. You can even choose "open awareness," in which you shine the spotlight on whatever arises in your consciousness. Although mindfulness meditation may be relaxing, it is aimed at producing awareness. In other words, it is aimed at falling awake, not asleep. But if you try a meditation and find yourself falling asleep, in keeping with the mindfulness approach you are to be accepting of that, not critical. Kindly self-compassion is central to mindfulness.

When you begin building your practice, several suggestions may be helpful. One is to use a quiet place where you won't be disturbed. Another is to build regularity into your practice by doing it at the same time each day. You can experiment with what time works best for you. Some people prefer to start their day with meditation, while others prefer it in the middle or at the end of the day. The meditative process is an empirical one — choose whatever you find most useful rather than what is recommended by the "authorities."

Without trying to change the thoughts and beliefs you have, mindfulness attempts to change your *relationship* to such thoughts. In this way, mindfulness approaches are sometimes termed *metacognitive*, because they pay attention to cognitive thought *processes* and not the thoughts themselves.

The metacognitive approach is key to how I work with people experiencing depression. Negative thoughts, beliefs, and feelings about oneself are very common in depression and are usually not valid — even the most firmly held beliefs. You may even be thinking this does not apply to you and that your negative thoughts are really accurate; we will take this up shortly.

As I mentioned in the Introduction, negative thoughts are not facts but rather symptoms of depression itself. For example, one young woman noted that whenever she felt depressed, she had the thought that no one cared about her. This depressive thought would escalate in intensity. When she emerged from depression, however, the thought diminished or disappeared. Clearly the thought was not a fact, but rather a symptom of her depression.

Vincent van Gogh, whose exact diagnosis remains imprecise, was thought to have had a mood disorder perhaps complicated by medication toxicity.[9] About his depressive episodes he said, "During the actual crises it seemed to me that everything I was imagining was reality."[10] After these episodes, he realized his thoughts were only transient products of his imagination — not facts.

Sometimes even therapists may not realize that such depressive thoughts are just mental events. For example, some individuals may castigate themselves after the death of a loved one: "If only I had gotten her to the doctor earlier," or "If only I had been home when he had his heart attack." Although in some instances it may be useful for a therapist to help a client unravel the origins of such guilty feelings, in the vast majority of situations this is a futile quest. It may be more useful to understand such guilty thoughts as symptoms of the depressive state itself.

In mindful approaches to depression, the key is not to find the origins of negative feelings, but to change your relationship to them, so they no longer have significant power in your life. When you find yourself feeling, "I am worthless," you will quickly be able to see that you are actually thinking, "I'm having the thought that I am worthless." You don't need to judge the validity of your thoughts, but rather just note them as transient mental events.

In mindful approaches to depression, the key is not to find the origins of negative feelings, but to change your relationship to them, so they no longer have significant power in your life.

A classic Buddhist cautionary tale describes a warrior who was shot by an enemy with a poisoned arrow. Before allowing the arrow to be removed, he asked, "Why is this happening to me? Who did this? Did I deserve this?" Understanding the answers to these questions is of little value compared to treating the actual injury. Pursuing the question of why something happened may in fact lead to delay and death in such a case. On the other hand, noticing the thoughts and associated feelings in the present moment as passing mental events and then making a skillful response may be the most liberating approach, as we will soon see.

Unlike other forms of therapy, the mindful approach represents a different way of living. It is about developing a lifestyle in which you gain some distance from your thoughts and feelings so you can gauge their validity. You may think your negative thoughts and feelings are true — that you are worthless, not as good as others, have some inherent defect, or will always be a failure. After all, the evidence for them has been with you for years! Or so you think. But your lens has been distorting your worldview.

Any distance from such thoughts allows you to begin responding differently. And that is the crux of MBCT: it enhances your ability to relate differently to your thoughts.

The fact that you chose to read this book is an important step along your life path, since it is an acknowledgment that you can change your relationship to depression. Changing the lens through which you see the world can affect your view of the future and your level of hope. If you are depressed, working your way through the book will require perseverance, but you have already taken the first step in reading this far.

PART
I

The Power of Now

2

WHAT MINDFULNESS IS AND WHAT IT IS NOT

There are various misconceptions about what mindfulness means. For example, some people mistakenly believe mindfulness involves emptying your mind of all thoughts. Mindfulness at its core is being aware of your experiences as you are experiencing them and suspending judgment about them. These include sensations, thoughts, and feelings.

The Time-Travel Problem

How many times have you tried to complete a task or search for something on the internet and found your mind wandering to the past or future? During a conversation, have you noticed how your mind travels to what you are going to say next rather than listening to what is being said? Our minds tend to veer away from the present moment and travel to the past and the future frequently. This time travel is a problem in both anxiety and depression; the mind tends to lock in on the future or the past. With anxiety you suffer excessive fear and worry, especially about the future. It may be a generalized sense of unease or focus more on a specific situation such as a social gathering or a phobic situation or object. A person with anxiety tends to anticipate future catastrophe.

With depression, you may share some of the concerns about the future and have anxious feelings, but you're also focused on the past. "I've always been depressed, and I'll never recover" (notice the focus on both the past and the future). But think about it. Did you ever feel that way before? Did you recover? Your mind then says, "But this time is different." The mindful approach focuses on what the suffering is like *in this moment* and lets go of projections about the future or feelings about the past. Can you accept your suffering in this moment, right now? If you can do that and stop forecasting the future, your current pain will diminish too.

With depression there is also an emphasis on past losses, failures, resentments, and regrets. If you are depressed, you may feel as if a loss has already occurred and you are trying to figure out what to do next. You may worry about these losses and catastrophes and find your mind going through endless loops of thinking about what happened. For example, you may have thoughts such as "How did this happen to me? What did I do to cause this? Did I deserve this because I failed somehow?" Such thinking, so common during depression, is called rumination.

Can you accept your suffering in this moment, right now? If you can do that and stop forecasting the future, your current pain will diminish too.

Rumination is the mind's attempt to solve insoluble problems. The thoughts that keep cycling through the mind during rumination are important drivers of depression. Depressed people tend to value the ruminations they have about the past as if they represented some form of emotional wisdom. They do not realize that the process often interferes with actual problem solving. Rumination has been identified as an important determinant of depression.

If you notice that you do this, you might try the following experiment. Give yourself fifteen minutes of full-strength rumination, and then check your mood. Typically, all that ruminating will lower your mood. You may think you are problem solving, telling yourself, "If I just thought more about this problem, I could prevent it from happening again in the future." This is not problem solving. True problem solving leads to an action and an improvement in mood and does not keep looping back on itself. Problem solving involves holding a difficulty in mind, considering a range of solutions, selecting the one most likely to succeed, and then acting on the solution.

Mindfulness can help you recognize rumination and then choose to disengage from it. When you notice rumination, you can frame it as such. If you are having trouble disengaging from ruminations and returning to a focus on the present moment, a technique that can be helpful is scheduling your ruminations. That is, you can let go of your ruminations right now by agreeing to do them at a particular time later: "I'll stop ruminating for now, but start it up again tonight at 8 PM." You can reassure yourself you are not going to relinquish your ruminations permanently, but are merely setting them aside for a certain time. Such a process helps you decenter from ruminative thoughts. You can more easily see that the thoughts do not represent your observing self and are not necessarily genuine facts. This in turn may lead to a change in the degree of belief about such thoughts.

Thoughts and moods are in constant conversation. Thinking of course often affects our mood. For example, a friend doesn't return your call in a timely way. You may think she doesn't like you anymore and your relationship is over. The outcome of such negative thoughts is a shift into a depressed or anxious mood. This process can also work in reverse. Feeling depressed or anxious can affect your thinking. Your mind will tend to generate even more negative or anxious thoughts, which in turn lead to further negative interpretations of what might otherwise be neutral events. Yes, negative thoughts often lead to downward shifts in mood, but alterations in mood may influence thoughts as well.

Mindfulness can help break this cycle of thought and mood interactions as well as prevent time travel to the future or the past. It is inherently useful when we are anxious or depressed, because it teaches us to focus on the present moment. It helps loosen the mind's focus on future catastrophes and past losses.

Relinquishing your focus on the past or the future has a natural antidepressant or anti-anxiety effect. For example, if you gently bring yourself back to the present moment and focus on your breath, you cannot also be ruminating about past events. By focusing on breath sensations, you limit your mind's capacity to be available for ruminating or catastrophizing. I'll be introducing some meditations to help train your mind to focus your awareness in later chapters.

As mentioned, mindfulness meditation can be thought of as shining the spotlight of attention on a specific focus that you select in the present moment. This spotlight can be as broad or narrow as you like. When beginning to develop a practice of mindfulness meditation, you may want to focus your attention on the breath, since it is usually a relatively neutral object of attention. You will notice that as you focus your attention, the mind calms.

A Buddhist saying maintains that if you have a glass of dirty water, it is hard to see through it. If you hold the glass steady and let the dirt settle, then the water clears and it is easier to see through. In a sense, we are often in an agitated state as a result of what is going on in our daily life, at work or in our relationships, and it is hard to see things clearly. As you start to steady your mind, you are able to see things more clearly.

Mindfulness builds this capacity to focus attention and eases you away from a tendency to ruminate. And this shift away from rumination in and of itself typically results in an improvement in mood. You may notice this effect when you try the next meditation and see what happens when you let go of rumination even for a few minutes. Try rating your rumination level on a 10-point scale before and after the mindfulness meditation. I'm willing to bet you will ruminate less after the meditation. This effect will grow as your practice progresses.

TRY THIS: This Present Moment

Sitting quietly in a comfortable, upright posture in a chair, allow your eyes to drift shut or gaze softly on the floor in front of you, and come to the present moment. Notice the sensations throughout your body. Notice the contact points your body makes with the chair.

Shift your attention to your breath. Notice the flow of breath in and out of your nostrils. Notice the slight air turbulence at the tip of the nose.

Then after a few minutes, shift your attention to the sounds around you. Notice the sounds in the distance, and then after a few minutes shift to the sounds nearby. In this way get a mental picture of the soundscape around you.

Then shift your attention again to becoming aware of thoughts emerging from your mind, noticing them arise and then drift away.

After a few minutes, open your eyes and bring your attention back to the room.

Our research has shown that mindfulness training significantly decreased rumination levels after four weeks and even more so after eight weeks of practice.[1] These shifts toward decreased rumination were seen in clinical measures as well as in brain areas shown in functional MRIs of the participants. We will discuss some of the brain changes associated with mindfulness training in more detail in a later chapter. But for now, we can say that depression is associated with decreased activation in the areas of the brain associated with emotion regulation. With mindfulness training these areas have increased activation, as if they are coming back online. An important point from these findings is that mindfulness practice is associated with measurable changes in brain function.

By focusing on the present moment, which is, after all, the only time we actually can control, many people experience a significant improvement in mood, with less anxiety and depression. In some instances, you can turn down the volume on the depressive voices from the past that are replaying in your head by allowing them simply to pass out of your consciousness, without becoming attached to them or attempting to dispute them. This process is something like window shopping as you walk down the street. You can notice the things being displayed, but you don't have to go in and buy them!

Whenever you find yourself replaying thoughts about something that happened in the past or getting anxious thinking about some encounter or event to come, just try to step away and look at what's happening. Try to bring your attention to what is happening right here, right now.

A pair of researchers in England did a particularly interesting study of individuals with various symptoms including depression. In that study, they had these individuals focus their attention on a particular sound for thirty minutes a day. By the end of the study, the participants' moods had improved dramatically.[2] This suggests that being able to break up depressive ruminations through focused attention may be an important healing factor.

Mindfulness Practices

Mindfulness is the practice of focusing the awareness on the present moment, and there are essentially two common ways of going about it. One is a discrete period of formal mindfulness practice like the one we did above, and the other is bringing mindful awareness to everyday life.

Formal mindfulness practice can be done in a variety of ways, such as sitting quietly for thirty minutes and focusing on your breath. This is the form of meditation that many people associate with the misconception I mentioned earlier, that meditation requires completely clearing the mind of all thoughts. Such a state of mind is very unlikely and rarely seen even in experienced meditators.

Emptying the mind is not the point. In fact, it's not possible. The mind will not relinquish its continuous production of randomly emerging thoughts as well as emotions and physical sensations. When you practice mindfulness meditation, however, you will notice that the mind can become steadier and able to focus on whatever it is you are selecting as the object of attention. So, as you approach the meditations I offer in this book, forget about "emptying your mind." It just doesn't work that way.

The Laboratory of Neuroimaging at the University of Southern California estimates that we each have thousands of thoughts per day. These range from specific conscious thoughts to processing multiple sensory stimuli. That's a lot of thoughts per minute! Our minds generate these thoughts throughout the day and night without any specific effort. It is as if our minds are popcorn poppers continually popping forth ideas, but sometimes doing so inconsistently, at different rates.

When suffering from depression, you may notice that the thoughts that do pop up are biased toward the negative, which means your mind may be bombarding you with pessimistic thoughts throughout much of the day. With such a self-induced negative public-relations campaign going on, it is easy to see how depression can be self-perpetuating.

Formal meditation exercises teach you techniques for dealing with the barrage of ideas going on constantly in the mind. You learn how to focus the attention in the present moment and disengage from, and so defuse, the mental chatter.

Besides sitting meditation or other specific types of meditation, another way to practice mindfulness is to incorporate it into your everyday life. For example, you can notice the sensations in your feet and legs while you walk. You can chop vegetables in the kitchen by focusing on the chopping process and bringing the attention back to this focus when you notice your mind wandering to rehashing an earlier conversation or fast-forwarding to some future dread. When you shower, you can just feel the hot water hitting your body and smell the soap. You can eat your food mindfully, doing it slowly, so you can actually taste and smell and experience what you are eating.

While attending a silent mindfulness retreat, I experimented with this awareness practice with a dessert consisting of rye toast, peanut butter, and raisins. I found I couldn't separate the tastes of this combination of foods, so I tried to mindfully eat a raisin by itself. I was astounded as I closed my eyes and tried to focus on the tastes and where they occurred in my mouth. I noticed that biting into the raisin released a sweet taste over the front of the tongue, just where the sweet taste buds are thought to be concentrated. I noticed the texture and the fragrance of the raisin. I was actually tasting a raisin for the first time in my life, instead of gobbling down a handful without awareness.

The idea with everyday mindfulness is to shine the spotlight of mindfulness on whatever you are engaged in in the present moment. Intentionally focusing the mind on an action or an object requires effort and a willingness to do so. When you begin, the meditations will often be more challenging than they will be after you've built up your skill set. As with most things, the more you practice, the easier it becomes.

Neither of these practices — formal mindfulness meditation or mindfulness in your everyday life — was developed as an anxiety and depression treatment. They were originally seen as part of a contemplative approach to life or a religious philosophy. It is only in the past few decades that their utility in this regard has been recognized. Throughout this book you'll be practicing harnessing mindfulness as a powerful application for regulating mood.

Interrupting Judgment and Evaluation

Mindfulness is about the awareness that comes from drawing attention to things in a nonjudgmental and nonevaluative way. For example, you may notice a pain in a part of your body. Instead of evaluating it as "terrible," "awful," or "cruel," the mindful approach suggests that you focus on the actual sensations present even before you label them as pain. This is what we mean when we say that mindfulness is about noticing things as they are without judging them. Mindfulness is focused on the present moment. It is released from the past or the future.

Mindfulness is focused on the present moment. It is released from the past or the future.

Winston Churchill is known as one of the great leaders of the twentieth century. Less well known is that he struggled with long-standing recurrent depression. In fact, Churchill would speak of his depression's return by saying, "My black dog is back." The term *black dog* is useful in considering how you might view depression. For example, instead of viewing the black dog as a terrifying beast, you could try looking at it as if for the first time. If you had no prior knowledge of or associations with black dogs and did not immediately anticipate being attacked, much of the emotional charge would be lifted. Imagine applying this to your depressive thoughts and feelings and viewing them with fresh eyes.

Humans and other sapient beings are hardwired to be on guard for potential threats. The mind has automatic reactions that can be very helpful. For example, when you are faced with a dangerous situation, such as a possible automobile accident, it may help you to respond instantaneously to the situation and avoid injury. However, in many nonemergency situations, where an urgent fight-or-flight response is not necessary, your mind may still react as if a threatening situation were present. This may lead to inappropriate depression or anxiety. This tendency is particularly prominent in individuals with depression, because there is a bias toward viewing things and recalling past events negatively. This frequently leads to distorted assessments of the current situation.

Humans, however, have a unique response to threats. Noted Stanford biologist Robert Sapolsky describes the differences between humans and animals in his book *Why Zebras Don't Get Ulcers*.[3] Zebras respond to a realistic threat such as a lion chasing them by activating a flight response and running away as fast as possible. Once they are safe, their blood pressure and pulse rapidly come back to normal. Unfortunately, in humans, this is often not the case. There can be a fight-or-flight response even when the threat is minimal or even only imagined. Furthermore, the physiological response to stress may continue long after the threat has diminished. This leads to a variety of pathological reactions in the body such as hypertension, tachycardia, and immune system changes.

In studies of brain function in depressed individuals, the primitive areas of the brain responsible for sending out the alarm warning of potential threats are extremely active. These areas remain active even when there is no realistic basis for an alarm. Mindfulness offers a way of disengaging from such thoughts and preventing a downward spiral into depression. With mindfulness practice, the alarm areas become less active and the perceived threats become less pressing.

Another exercise that is useful in keeping you from judging or evaluating negative thoughts and feelings is the alien analogy. Imagine that you are an alien visiting earth. If you were to drop down to earth and experience what you are experiencing now, what would it be like? How would depression feel to an alien who dropped into your body? Remember, the alien does not know your personal history and has no basis on which to judge the thoughts and sensations; the alien can only describe them: "Oh, there's a thought about...How interesting."

I find that the alien perspective can also be applied to everyday experiences to shift you toward being more mindful. As you go about your day, imagine that you are an alien visiting earth just for today. Tomorrow you will be transported to a new planet. How does that affect your viewpoint?

If you are leaving tomorrow, is somebody's negative comment so bothersome? Does the model of the car you drive make much of a difference if you are going to leave it behind tomorrow? Might you be kinder in your interactions if you're just passing through? Do the worries you have about the future make much sense? Do you need to hang on to past injustices? Do you want to be happy or unhappy during your one-day trip to earth? Having a mindfulness perspective gives you the freedom to make that choice.

Say you are driving down the middle lane of an interstate highway and enjoying your day. A driver from the left lane cuts in front of you to take the exit in the right lane. You have to slow down abruptly, but no damage occurs. You immediately get angry. Your heart starts to race as your mind develops scenarios about why the incident occurred. "Did the driver mean to upset me? Was the person devaluing me as a driver?" You might allow your initial anger to build, perhaps affecting you for some time afterward.

But what do you really know about what happened? The fact of the event is that, in a split second, another driver cut in front of you. All the rest of it is your mind generating thoughts. As you view your thoughts, you may become aware of other possibilities. Perhaps the other driver was sick or a student driver. You get to decide whether you will let the anger simmer with the initial thoughts, shift to less anger-producing ones, or simply withdraw your attention and focus on your driving and being happy — it's your one day on earth after all. Do you want to allow your happiness to depend on someone else's actions? Yes, easier said than done, and that's why we call it practice.

Another way of understanding how mindfulness, in focusing on the present moment, enables you to gain some distance from your thoughts is to consider how it may apply to suffering in depression. Picture yourself in the middle of a bout of depression. You might say to yourself, "I can't stand this," "I can't go on like this," or "This will lead to disaster for me and my family." These are examples of how we project into the future and suffer because of it. But in each case that's a choice.

I had a clear illustration of this when I had a severe headache. For me, a headache often accompanied a depressive period. I felt significant pain and thought I could not stand it any longer. I wondered how I would fulfill obligations in the coming days if the pain persisted and fantasized embarrassing failures at several upcoming speaking engagements. A mindful perspective allowed me to realize that I was in fact "standing" this pain in the present moment. If I could keep my focus on the *present moment*, I could let go of worry about future catastrophes. In fact, research by Melissa Day and Beverly Thorn in Australia has demonstrated that MBCT training helped headache sufferers reduce pain intensity, pain interference with activities, and pain catastrophizing.[4]

Mindfulness helps you let go of how things might be in the future and come back to focusing on just this moment. You don't have to hypothesize about the future; just keep coming back to the present moment. What is actually happening right now? Focus on the bodily sensations, thoughts, and feelings — but less as a subject and more as an observer noting what is present.

The more you can do this — focus your attention on the present, letting go of the past and future — the more you will feel the natural antidepressant effects of mindfulness.

As I have mentioned, one of the difficulties with depression is that not only do we have a tendency to make critical evaluations and judgments, but we accept them as if they are facts. For example, I might think that the person who refused a request I made at a store didn't like me. When I remember my mindfulness training and refrain from evaluating, it occurs to me that she might be merely following company procedures. Mindfulness focuses on being nonjudgmental and nonevaluative toward others and others' actions as well as toward yourself. For example, you might judge yourself as weak because you are depressed. A less judgmental view might be that you are like millions of other people in the world who share a similar illness.

One of the difficulties with depression is that not only do we have a tendency to make critical evaluations and judgments, but we accept them as if they are facts.

It's important to note the difference between evaluations and descriptions of fact. There was an old television show, *Dragnet*, which featured detective Sergeant Friday, who always insisted, "Just the facts, ma'am," in his interviews with witnesses. He was seeking a description of evidence and not an evaluation. That's our aim here too — description without judgment or evaluation. For example, look at a table in your house or office. A description of it would be: "That's a brown table." An evaluation would be: "That's a beautiful brown table" or "That's an inadequate table." The last two statements are evaluations — opinions — not facts.

The tendency to dish out harsh self-criticisms expressed as facts is often prominent in depression. Shifting to a more mindful style brings you closer to evaluating yourself and others in a cooler, more factual way, closer to describing what is present without judgment or criticism, and closer to just accepting what is.

Bringing Attention Back to What Is

Mindfulness meditation consists of focusing on an object of attention, noticing when your mind has wandered off and become involved in an emerging thought, feeling, or bodily sensation, and then bringing the attention back to the object of attention. These three elements are always present. Even when you've been practicing for a long time, your mind will continue to generate distractions (such as thoughts) regularly. You must continually notice when this happens, let go of the distraction, and gently return the focus to the object of attention.

You might think of the mind as a puppy that often wanders off. If you harshly yank the puppy back to your side, it may start to wander off more frequently. If you gently bring it back to what you're focusing on, it is more likely to stay. In depression, the puppy often brings back something we don't want, such as a past failure or pending catastrophe. But we don't have to be angry with the puppy. It's just what puppies do, and getting angry may only make it want to wander away more often. If you gently bring your attention back to the meditation object, such as the breath, and become kinder and gentler with your mind, it may stop wanting to wander so much.

With practice, however, it will become easier to observe distracting thoughts as they emerge and then let them fade out of awareness. By learning how to let go of diversionary stimuli, you can train yourself to become less at the mercy of depressive thoughts. One MBCT participant observed, "When I'm meditating on my breath and I can let go of thoughts about what I'm going to have for dinner, then I can let go of some of my depressive thoughts too."

As you develop your mindfulness skills, you will notice you can observe sensations, thoughts, and feelings without feeling a need to react immediately to them. You can also begin to apply your growing skills outside of the specific meditations. You can bring your mindfulness into everyday life. You can become aware of what the sensations are in your feet as you walk along the ground. You can become aware of what the sensations are like in your mouth as you brush your teeth or on your back as the warm water flows over you in the shower. As you begin to notice how you can shine the spotlight of mindfulness onto many activities, you can become aware that being mindful is not confined to sitting still and focusing on your breath.

Now let's try a mindfulness meditation similar to my raisin experience. You can repeat this meditation with other everyday activities by attempting to do them from a mindful perspective. Just begin to notice the sensations associated with, for example, bathing, brushing your teeth, eating different foods, or performing household tasks. Observe the physical sensations, the smells, the tastes, the sounds.

TRY THIS: Eating Mindfully

Choose a food item to eat, sit at the table, and close your eyes.

Bring the food toward your mouth. Notice that you can begin to smell the food, and that you start to salivate as if your mouth knows what to do with the food.

Place the food in your mouth and roll your tongue around it, noticing what it feels like, the textures and the sensations of the food.

Then slowly bite into the food, and notice what flavors occur and where. Taste buds of different types are located throughout the mouth, particularly in different regions of the tongue. As you begin to let the juices of the food flow over these areas, notice specifically what areas of the mouth and tongue are activated by eating this food. Are the sweet juices more active on the tip of the tongue? Are salty juices more prominent on the sides?

In this way you deepen your awareness of the food and notice things that are impossible to appreciate when you're eating in a less mindful way.

The following story illustrates the utility of mindfulness practice and the idea that it may be preferable to learn how to respond skillfully to stressful situations rather than expect them to disappear. They say that a wanderer with bare feet developed cuts and bruises on his feet from the stones and rocks he walked on. He prayed to a wise man he encountered to have the world covered in leather, so that he would not continue to damage his feet. The wise man replied that it would take less leather to cover the wanderer's feet than it would to cover the world. As the poet Rumi wrote, "Yesterday I was clever, so I wanted to change the world. Today I am wise, so I am changing myself."

Bhante Gunaratana, in his book *Mindfulness in Plain English*, gives what for us can serve an elegant description of the first steps of mindfulness. He says mindfulness is being able to "realize what you are doing as you are doing it" and then "stand back and quietly watch.... Learn to watch the arising of thought and perception with a feeling of serene detachment. We learn to view our own reactions to stimuli with calmness and clarity. We begin to see ourselves reacting without getting caught up in the reactions themselves."[5]

This skill of mindfulness leads to being able to observe yourself and decenter from your thoughts. In depression, the self often fuses or identifies with negative thoughts coming from the mind; it believes those thoughts are true facts and becomes invested in them. Taking a mindful approach allows the self to step back and observe that they are nothing but transient mental events with no inherent validity. They are like soap bubbles rising to the surface and then drifting away from consciousness. When negative thoughts are seen this way, their power is greatly diminished.

Here is a meditation you can use to practice decentering from your thoughts. By the way, it highlights the difference between mindfulness meditation and traditional cognitive therapy; in the latter you have to weigh whether a thought is accurate or valid and try to come up with an alternative. If you've been hanging on to negative thoughts for many years, it may be difficult to change the thought content. Mindfulness is focused on changing your relationship to your thoughts, not the content.

TRY THIS: Drifting Clouds

Sit quietly, with eyes closed, focusing on your breath for a few minutes.

Then imagine yourself watching clouds drifting across the sky. Picture the clouds as representing your thoughts drifting into and then out of your awareness. The sky represents your observing self. Can you watch the thoughts fade into the distance without attaching to them?

After five minutes, bring your attention back to your setting.

Stop Believing Your Thoughts

Some people have said that depression can be considered a discrepancy-based disorder in which individuals compare themselves negatively to others or to some idealized self. They might say, "I'm not as smart (or desirable or beautiful or wealthy, etc.) as..." With such preconceptions, when you get involved in a work setting or personal relationship, you expect to be rejected. In this scenario, when others discover how incompetent or undesirable you are, why wouldn't they reject you?

This type of belief is one that is often so deeply held that is called a core or central belief of the individual. It organizes virtually all the ways of interacting in relationships in both work and social settings. It colors your worldview and the future. You see the world pessimistically and as headed toward a grim future.

You may be so driven by such thoughts that even the best traditional cognitive therapy can't unseat them. With the mindful approach, however, you can realize that such self-critiques are just thoughts and they do not have to be believed. They come into awareness and then move out of awareness. In other words, you can loosen and shift your stance toward these beliefs. Over time, you may begin to have fewer negative evaluations and judgments, but the important element is that you do not have to hold them so firmly when they do occur.

Several observers, such as mindfulness teacher Joseph Goldstein and psychologist Steven C. Hayes, describe thoughts using the analogy of a freight train. In this analogy, if you hop on the freight train, there is no telling where you will end up. If you suffer from depression, there is a good chance that hopping on the train will take you to a town called Depression. If you are able to watch the train cars go by without hopping on, you may be able to stay relatively free of depressive destinations. When you observe the freight cars going by, you are allowing your observing self to see the bigger picture of the world and not getting attached to any particular thought. You are beginning to develop a broader view of your own skills and your ability to observe your mental processes.

You can conceptualize your observing self as that which observes your mind. Your mind in turn is aware of your bodily sensations and your mental events — your thoughts and feelings. Your observing self watches the mind having thoughts, feelings, and bodily sensations. Doing so gives you a broader perspective and awareness of the mental events that are occurring. For example, notice when you might say something to yourself such as "I'm worthless." Actually, you can notice several things about this. One is that such a comment is a self-judgment, and self-judgments are a common thought loop in depression.

Second, the comment is actually a thought — "I am having the thought that I'm worthless." That reframing changes the comment from a factual statement into another transient mental event. It may *seem* more factual, because that is the distortion that depression brings — a sense of certitude about negative self-judgments. If your thoughts had colors, self-judgments would be glowing in bright, vivid hues, so certain are you of them, in comparison to the subdued tones of more neutral thoughts — but they are all just colors.

The ability to shift into the observing role can change your relationship to depression and pain in general. For example, once I was having a severe migraine that had lasted for more than a day. I again tried shifting to the present moment. Moreover, this time I tried shifting into the observer-self mode. I said to myself that I could see Stu suffering a headache, almost as if I was observing someone else right next to me telling me he had a headache. I could be compassionate toward him for his suffering, but the pain was somewhat removed from my observing self. This changed the perspective dramatically.

Thoughts and mood have important interactions. Psychologists Albert Ellis and later Aaron Beck elucidated a model of these interactions, the ABC model. In this conceptualization A represents an activating event, B is a belief or thought about the event, and C is the emotional consequence of the belief, the resulting mood. Most people assume that there is a direct line from A to C, that it is the activating event that results in their mood change. In fact, it is the intervening step, B, the *belief* about the event, that determines how they will end up feeling, not A, the actual event.

Usually it is a bit more difficult to become aware of the belief that is stimulating the mood, but with some attention it can become clear. For example, I observe two coworkers talking and then one looks my way. I may feel upset observing this. What is important in determining my mood will be the belief I have about what is going on with my coworkers. If I think I am being talked about or left out of something, I may feel sad or betrayed. If I don't see their interactions as relating to me, my mood may not change at all. In this model, it is the belief that mediates the potential change in mood. The Greek philosopher Epictetus described a similar process when he wrote: "Men are disturbed not by things, but by the view which they take of them."

In depressive disorders there is tendency for beliefs to be biased toward the negative. A neutral or even positive event then may be interpreted negatively. A depressed mood can result from negative interpretations, but it can also then go on to generate negative thoughts unconnected to any precipitating event. When a depressed person is viewing the world through a negative lens, thoughts about self, past, and future are all distorted. The negative thoughts and beliefs are themselves symptoms of the illness. Mindfulness helps change the lens even momentarily.

Challenging negative thoughts is often difficult, because in order to change your thought you have to push off from the original thought. This process is illustrated in the mind experiment of trying not to think of something. Thus, trying to suppress or counter a negative thought may actually reinforce the negative thought. In mindfulness approaches, you do not have to challenge the thought at all. You let the thought go and realize it's merely a mental event. In depression, you can begin to recognize the maladaptive thoughts as just thoughts, and as soon as you do, you change your relationship to them rather than acting on them or believing that they are true. One member of a new MBCT group voiced a concern that she was not as good or "cool" as other members, because she was the only one wearing white shoes! As we explored this, it became possible for her to see that this was a thought and not a fact — an evaluative opinion that had little support in reality.

One woman in our program began to notice that she repeatedly said things to herself like, "What a dummy I am," "How incompetent I am," or "How inferior I am compared to everybody else." She noticed she repeated these evaluations of herself frequently throughout the day. She was amazed by how constant this barrage was, and she could begin to see the impact of these thoughts on her emotional life. She was starting to become aware of her thinking process. As she became aware, she became better able to let the thoughts go without engaging with them to try to either suppress or disprove them.

You may notice that such thoughts are often lurking nearby throughout the day and that they emerge into consciousness even when you are not thinking about anything negative at the time. Sometimes these thoughts are called *automatic negative thoughts*. They often include ideas about defects in oneself or a delusion of unworthiness. The important feature of mindfulness is that your observing self, which we will discuss in more detail in a later chapter, can help you *recognize that these thoughts are transient mental events* and *allow you to gain distance from them*. This is what we call the process of *decentering* from such thoughts or feelings.

Mindfulness allows the process to unfold. This means you can begin to see your thoughts as just thoughts. There may be a wide variety of passing thoughts ranging from memories to planning to fantasizing. In depression, judging and self-criticism are two common types of thoughts, but they need to be placed in the same category as all the others; they are just thoughts. You can try an experiment.

TRY THIS: Floating Leaves

Close your eyes and focus on the breath moving in and out.

When you are settled, picture yourself sitting on the bank of a slow-moving river. Imagine there are leaves drifting down the river and that each one represents a thought. Notice as each leaf comes into focus and then drifts away. You don't have to jump on the leaf or attach to it; just notice it.

Then observe what type of thought it is, such as planning, worrying, remembering, judging, or self-criticizing. When you notice the judging or self-criticizing thoughts, observe that they are thoughts just like all the others. Sometimes these thoughts have a voice or tone like that of someone from your past, but the thoughts are not people speaking; they are still just thoughts. In fact, thoughts just emerge into your consciousness like the leaves coming into your field of vision. In this sense, thoughts are not personal, and you don't have to take them as if they are.

Psychiatrist Mark Epstein has written of this process in his book *Thoughts Without a Thinker*.[6] Thoughts are like the noises in our environment that arise and fade away. They may be pleasant or unpleasant, but they aren't aimed at us.

In summary, mindfulness can best be thought of as a way of being, a skillful way of moving through life. Although you can practice it as a discrete form such as a body scan, which we will describe in the next chapter, you can also practice as you walk along a sidewalk or carry out a kitchen chore. Shining your mindfulness spotlight on whatever you like allows you to view thoughts and feelings from a decentered stance — from the observing self.

3 HOW MINDFULNESS HELPS IN DEPRESSION

Several components of mindfulness play a particular role in helping to heal depression. First is the mindfulness focus of being in the present moment. When we are focused on the present, we have less bandwidth available to ruminate about past failures or future catastrophes. Another feature of mindfulness that allows you to cope with depression is decentering. Decentering allows you to gain distance from depressive thoughts and feelings. We'll look at this process further in the next chapter.

> *Decentering allows you to gain distance from depressive thoughts and feelings.*

Thoughts as Symptoms of Depression

Research has shown that a number of thoughts are common to individuals with depression. These negative thoughts can be considered symptoms of depression. For any one individual, however, there are a smaller number of thoughts that are specific to that individual. You may notice that certain thoughts are typical for you when you become depressed. These thoughts form your depressive signature. They represent your symptom pattern just as much as early awakening, loss of appetite, or loss of enjoying activities you previously enjoyed are part of your particular depressive pattern.

One exercise to help you decenter from such thoughts is to make a list of the top ten most common thoughts that occur when you are depressed. It may be useful to include on your list thoughts that you tend to believe very strongly when you are depressed and that you don't believe as strongly when you're feeling better. If you can identify these thoughts, you will be able to decenter from them more easily, because you know they are symptoms of your depression rather than immutable facts.

Paradoxically, thoughts that we most firmly believe are often the least likely to be true. For example, many depressed people hold on tightly to beliefs such as "I am defective," "I am unlovable," "I will never be successful," or "The world is doomed to disaster." These types of thoughts are cognitive symptoms that occur as commonly in depression as a fever occurs as a symptom of an infection. Although people suffering from depression tend to believe these negative thoughts to be true, these thoughts are just as much part of the phenomenon of depression as bodily symptoms such as a change of appetite or sleep pattern.

One way of testing whether a thought is a fact or a symptom of depression is to do an experiment. If you temporarily see that thought as a fact, does it lead to healing and peace or pain and suffering? If you are having a thought that leads to worsened depression, that is a good clue that it is related to the depression itself and is not an actual fact. You do not have to ask anyone else, just yourself, "How do I feel after thinking the thought?"

If you have trouble letting go of the idea that your thought is not in fact true, that is because you are having trouble seeing it as just a thought. Another way to investigate whether a thought is true is to inquire if the thought often repeats. If so, that is another good clue that it is part of a story you've constructed. Once you recognize this, it's amazing how its power diminishes. It tends to lose its hold over you.

Many people get stuck over this notion of truth versus judgment when looking at their thoughts. What if someone says, "I am fat," and he actually is obese? That is a fact, yes, but in depressive states this is often where the thinking shifts quickly toward defeat — "I can't do anything about it" — and the mood worsens. In the case of the obese person, with a mindfulness perspective he can gain some distance from the thought that he is overweight, which will allow him to respond skillfully — in this case to shift out of helplessly being doomed to obesity and instead searching out a diet and exercise program that will work for him. Judgment gives way to self-compassionate action.

Depression tends to cause cascades of negative thoughts. Using mindfulness and observing that your mind is generating these thoughts allows you to start changing your relationship to them. For example, when feeling like a failure, you might say, "There's that failure type of thought again," and in that way be able to let it go or lessen its grip.

In one instance a woman described feeling depressed after being fired from a job after several years because she was frequently argumentative. In fact, in the mindfulness class she was often argumentative as well. She was encouraged to observe her argumentative thoughts in her meditation and to try letting them go and noticing how she felt. When she did so, she noticed she felt very vulnerable. She realized this perceived vulnerability was related to some past events in her childhood, but she no longer was as helpless as she had been as a child. She gradually was able to loosen up her argumentative style and stay more rooted in the present moment.

The Stories We Create

A meditation teacher at a well-known meditation center had suffered from occasional depression. He described the walking meditation that he was doing outside in front of the meditation center's main building. He would walk back and forth, paying attention to the sensations he was experiencing in his lower limbs from his feet to his hips as he walked. When his mind wandered, he would notice the wandering and bring his attention back to the lower limbs. At the time that he was doing this, a highly esteemed lama from Tibet was visiting the meditation center. As the teacher was walking back and forth, he happened to look up and see the lama watching him from the second-story window.

The teacher continued walking back and forth, glancing up regularly to see if the lama was still in the window. The lama continued to watch as the teacher carried out his walking meditation. The teacher began to wonder what he was doing wrong: "Why is he so concerned with me? What am I failing at?" Finally, after the forty-five-minute meditation session ended, the teacher went inside and up to the second floor to see the lama. He discovered that he had not been seeing the lama at all, but rather a coatrack that he had misinterpreted from the ground as being the lama looking out at him and finding fault with the way he was doing his meditation.

You see, even the most experienced meditator can create a false story to explain his perceptions! This is what our minds do. They create stories. This helps us feel secure that we understand what is happening in the world around us, and it can be very useful at times. The trouble is, for those of us with depressive disorders it is very likely that our stories will be negative and not an accurate reflection of reality.

Do you notice how you often choose a movie that is just like ones you have seen before? You may be drawn to dramas, action films, romances, comedies, or thrillers. In real life, we also tend to create stories that follow familiar themes. For example, in depression we may expect that someone will betray or reject us. We may imagine we will be found to be defective. We have a tendency to operate as if the theme that we selected is real and forget that we have brought our own theme to the party. Similarly, we may interact with colleagues or romantic partners as if they were figures based on old movies with familiar plots without realizing we wrote those dramas ourselves!

A forty-five-year-old man in one of my groups talked about the fact that he was never able to find a satisfactory romantic partner. He always felt betrayed by the women he became involved with. He also told a story from his teen years when he was in the kitchen with his stepfather and mother during an argument. His stepfather struck him in the face and knocked him to the floor. His mother walked out of the room and did not return for several hours. The man never got over feeling betrayed by his mother.

As he became more mindful, he began to see alternate explanations for his mother's behavior in this story he had carried with him into his adult relationships. Perhaps his mother had been trying to cool off the situation by leaving (there was no further violence). Perhaps she was so frightened for herself that she could not tolerate being in the room. Whatever the facts of the case were, the story line of betrayal that he had carried for many years was only one of several possibilities. As he began to look back at his relationships with women, he could see other possibilities besides the perceived betrayals as well.

Another client, a thirty-five-year-old woman, often felt sure that she was going to be rejected in her relationships with men. She would expect this and, even shortly after meeting them, would react as if the rejection had already occurred. As she began practicing mindfulness, she came to realize that the idea that she was being rejected was not a fact or an eventuality, but just a thought, one that stemmed from the disappointment she had experienced as a teenager in her first serious relationship. This became evident to her as she developed new relationships and compared her automatic thought to a more decentered view of what might be happening. For example, when she was out on a date and her date checked his watch, it might be because he wanted to know the time and not because he was bored with her.

You might think of your stream of negative thoughts as similar to a television with the horror channel always on. The input from this channel has a way of coloring all your experience. But realizing it is the depression channel and that there are other options you can change to can be liberating. It requires courage to make the change, because the original channel may be rooted much earlier in life; it is so familiar. In fact, you may not be able to change the channel, but mindfulness offers you the opportunity to change *your relationship* to the channel. The same shows may be playing, but you don't have to pay as much attention to them. They can be relegated to the background, so that unpleasant thoughts do not have to occupy center stage in your life.

Chicken or Egg?

Sure, sometimes it is negative thoughts that lead to depression, but when we are depressed, we tend to become negative-thought machines. Many of our negative thoughts are derived from the depressive state itself. For example, the thought "I am defective in some fundamental way" often occurs when you are feeling depressed. However, if you can recall a time when you were not feeling so depressed, you might remember that you didn't feel so defective then. This illustrates clearly that the belief is not a fact, but rather a negative thought flowing from the depression.

Our thoughts and beliefs are quite variable depending on our mood. The effect of depression on our thinking is that we believe certain things to be concrete facts that are really not facts at all, no matter how true they seem. We see this in psycholog- ical experiments where negative mood inductions, such as listening to somber music or viewing di- saster images, can profoundly affect what type of thoughts occur. Our minds are so easily in- fluenced, and negative thoughts are common manifestations of depression.

Many of our negative thoughts are derived from the depressive state itself.

One woman became so full of despair that she thought she should tell her psychiatrist to give up on her. Once she started exploring her thoughts and feelings mind- fully, she felt an improvement. It took a few weeks, but she was able to change her relationship to her depression. In fact, she began to call depression her friend, because she realized it was calling her attention to a life situation she had not been facing. She had been stuck in an abusive relationship and had thought there was nothing to be done about it, when in fact there were a number of alternate courses of action. Once she had developed a decentered view of her depression, she could see that it had wo- ken her up to her life. And once she realized this, her mood began to lift.

How Does Mindfulness Help?

Although there is considerable discussion about how mindfulness exerts its effect, there appear to be several important potential mechanisms. One is that it gives you the ability to *focus your at- tention in an intentional way*. Bringing your attention to bear on a particular point of interest may have a beneficial effect on your mood. For example, mindful focusing on body sensations, sounds, or your thoughts (as just thoughts) may help reduce depression.

Another way that mindfulness helps counter depression is

that it *interrupts rumination.* In my own studies of depressed individuals, rumination levels decreased significantly with eight weeks of mindfulness training.

In depression, people have high levels of ruminative thoughts typically focused on the past, on regrets. Since you can't go back in time to redo things, such ruminative thoughts only lead to disappointment. It is like hoping to have a better past and not recognizing that the past is already written. Some people remain locked into efforts to rectify the past and produce a different outcome without recognizing that that is not possible.

Mindfulness also gives you the *tools to respond more skillfully to self-critical thoughts*, rather than just being at their mercy. One tool is to label the critic: "Ah, there you are, my judgmental old friend, making your comments again." Once you notice them, try injecting some humor or sarcasm: "Don't know what I'd do without your critiques!"

Another tool is to actually keep a running count of how many self-critical thoughts you have in a day. One woman did this and reported she had several hundred. She realized that with this internal melody, it was no wonder she felt so poorly about herself!

Picture the critical thoughts as clouds drifting across your consciousness until they disappear from view. As you become more experienced with this approach, the critical thoughts can become more like background noise, not inhabiting the forefront of your awareness.

Another common mechanism of mindfulness is *decentering*, which involves being able to stand apart from our thoughts and view them calmly and clearly. This can take a number of forms. Observing your thoughts and realizing that you're having them is one example of decentering. Reframing the phrase "I am worthless" to "I'm having the thought that I am worthless" is an example of decentering. It produces a dramatic shift in stance. You relate to the thought with less absolute self-condemnation.

Even observing that you are in a certain mood or feeling state can be powerful. For example, switching from the thought "I am depressed" to "I am having the feeling that I am depressed" gives you a certain freedom about how you're going to respond to the situation. By viewing your thoughts and feelings from a greater distance, they become less compelling. This decentering fostered by MBCT has been shown by Ramona Kessel and colleagues to be associated with decreased severity of depression.[1]

Thoughts are not facts, including the ones that seem as though they are. Critical thoughts, which are so common in depression, can be viewed as "the critic's channel" or the critical voice. Next time your mind wanders to thoughts such as "I'm a terrible person," "I am a failure," or "I am a terrible meditator," try reframing these thoughts as merely your inner critical voice, not absolute judgments of fact.

> Thoughts are not facts, including the ones that seem as though they are.

Basic Mindfulness: The Body Scan

The mind frequently wanders during meditation, and understanding that this is a natural quality of the mind can help you to become gentler with yourself. For example, the mind is often distracted by sounds. One way of dealing with this is to notice when the mind is wandering in response to various sounds and use that recognition as a way to bring your focus back to the object of attention, such as your breath. The distraction itself can help you sharpen your attention.

The following meditation is best done by listening to the script on the website or downloaded to your listening device; alternately, you can have a friend read it to you. You can do this meditation either lying down or sitting in a chair, and you might eventually try both positions to see what works best for you.

TRY THIS: Body Scan

Come to a comfortable position either sitting upright in a chair or lying down.

Allow your eyes to drift shut whenever you're ready, if you feel comfortable doing so, or else gaze softly in front of you.

Begin by focusing on the breath moving in and out through the nostrils. Feel the breath as it moves in and out, and then notice how you can follow the breath as it moves through the upper airways and then down into the chest and lungs. Feel how the chest and lungs expand with each breath in and fall with each breath out. Then let go of that region.

Bring the attention in the present moment to the abdomen. Select a spot on the abdominal wall and notice how the cycle of the breath creates sensations at that spot. You can feel your abdomen rise with each breath in and fall with each breath out. This is due to diaphragmatic breathing, in which the diaphragm moves down with each in-breath and up with each out-breath.

Now let that region fade, and bring the attention to the toes of the left foot. Notice what's present there, various sensations such as moisture, warmth, coolness, tingling. Just notice what's there, and then expand the awareness to include the sole and heel of the left foot. Notice any contact points of the foot with the floor or mat that you may be lying on.

Next expand the awareness to include the entire left foot. Feel the breath moving in and out of the body part you are focusing your attention on.

Allow the foot to fade into the past, and then bring the attention to the left lower leg. Notice whatever is present there — contact points, muscular sensations — just notice what is present.

Let that fade, and bring the attention to the left knee, noticing whatever is present there, such as joint sensations, aching, or numbness.

Let that fade, and bring the attention to the left upper leg. Notice the sensations there, particularly in the large muscles of the upper leg. Are there contact points, pressure sensations?

Then, letting that region fade, bring the attention to the toes of the right foot. Notice the sensations there. Tingling, numbness, coolness, warmth?

Then expand the awareness to include the sole and heel of the right foot. Observe what is present there.

Then expand your awareness to include the entire right foot. Notice the sensations there.

Allow that region to fade, bring the attention to the right lower leg, and observe whatever is present there. As you observe, just notice what is there without any judgment, criticism, or evaluation.

Then allow that region to fade, bring the attention to the right knee, and notice the sensations that are present there, joint sensations, aching, or perhaps the breath moving in and out.

Let that region fade, bring the attention to the right upper leg, and notice the sensations there, perhaps warmth, muscle sensations, contact points with the mat or chair.

Then let that region fade, and bring the attention to the hips and pelvis, noticing whatever is present there.

Then let that region fade, bring the attention to the lower back, and notice the sensations there. Sometimes that region holds tension in the large muscles alongside the spine. See if you notice this, without trying to change it in any way. Just notice whether it is present or not.

Then shift the attention to the mid and upper back, and notice what is present here: contact points, pressure sensations, or muscular tension.

Then shift the attention again, to the left fingers and hand, noticing whatever is present in that region: tingling, numbness, pressure sensations, coolness, or warmth.

Let that region fade, and bring the attention to the left wrist, forearm, and elbow. Notice what is present in that area, joint sensations, pressure sensations, muscular tension, just accepting whatever is present.

Then let that region fade, and bring the attention to the left upper arm and shoulder. Notice what is present here, joint sensations, pressure sensations, accepting whatever's present without trying to change it, just observing.

Then, letting that region fade, bring the attention to the right hand and fingers. Notice what is present here, tingling, numbness, pulsing. Just notice what is present, and accept it as it is.

Then, letting that region fade, bring the attention to the right wrist, forearm, and elbow. Notice the sensations present here, such as contact points, pressure, muscular tension, or joint sensations.

Then let that region fade, and bring the attention to the right upper arm and shoulder. Notice muscular sensations, temperature sensations, and joint sensations.

Then let that region fade, and bring the attention to the neck and shoulder area. Notice if there's muscular tension or relaxation alongside the spine in the neck. Accept whatever is present without trying to change it.

Then bring the attention to the scalp and notice if there are any contact points or pressure areas and whether the small, fine muscles of the face are loose, limp, or tight.

Then return the focus to the nose, feeling the breath moving in and out again through the nostrils. Notice the turbulence at the tip of the nostrils from the air moving in and out. Notice the air moving out of the nostrils is warmer than the air moving in.

When you're ready, bring the attention back to the room.

What did you notice when you were doing this meditation? It's not unusual for some people to fall asleep during the body scan, but others are surprised to see how frequently the mind wanders from the object of attention, as they go through the different parts of the body. The mind wanders during meditation. That is what our minds do.

The intent of the body scan is to focus attention on bodily sensations, but noticing when the mind wanders is an important part of the meditation as well. When this occurs, gently congratulate yourself for having noticed that your mind wandered and then bring the attention back. In essence, it is an accomplishment to notice that your mind has wandered. Many people have the misconception that in meditation you must lock your mind on one single point and if it does not stay there, you are not meditating correctly; this is not true. Mindfulness means focusing on a particular object of attention, but knowing that your mind is likely to wander, then noticing that, and then in a kind and gentle way bringing your attention back to the object.

Sometimes people with depression react to meditation in ways that are related to their illness. For example, although anyone learning a new skill might question whether they are doing it "right," if you are depressed, you may be *sure* you are doing it wrong and, importantly, believe you won't be able to learn how to do it in the future. This is based on the faulty view that there is a right way to do this.

Every time you go through this meditation, just like everybody else, you will have a different experience. As they say, no one walks in the same river twice, meaning that there is always a new flow in the river, and a person will always have a new experience. This is completely true of mindfulness meditation, especially in doing the body scan. As you are going through it, you may notice how your mind wanders quite freely on one day, whereas on another day when you tried it, you had much less wandering. This is completely normal. If you have the thought that you are not doing it right or that you are deficient in doing it, there is a very good chance that this thought is your depression speaking. The key element is not whether your mind wanders from the object of attention to other thoughts or feelings or even if you fall asleep. The important issue is how you respond to what you've noticed.

Wandering thoughts present a wonderful opportunity for practicing the skill of altering your relationship to your thoughts. For example, if you have the thought while you're doing the body scan that you are deficient at doing it compared to other people, you can label it "an evaluation thought" and then return the attention back to the object of attention without engaging with it. In other words, if you notice you're having a thought like that, you can allow yourself to let go of it and bring the attention back to the object, whatever body part you are focused on at that time. In this way, you begin to build skill in being able to let go of thoughts. Virtually no one can do the body scan with no mind wandering at all. When your mind wanders, you can redirect your attention in a compassionate manner.

The meditation presents a good opportunity for watching the ways in which your mind wanders. One way to facilitate redirecting your attention is to label what the distraction has been. For example, if you start to have a planning thought about what you need to do later in the day, you can just label that as a planning thought, file it away, and bring the attention back to the body part you are focusing on. If you notice that you're having a worrying thought about something that has already happened, you can label it as "worry thought" or "rumination" and then let it go, while drawing the attention back to the intended focus.

Occasionally you may notice that you develop an itch while doing the body scan. The itch feels very compelling, and you typically have an urge to scratch it. Before immediately scratching that itch, you can instead shine the light of mindfulness on it, noticing what the sensations are like, such as tingling, numbness, or tickling. As you notice the sensations, you may have a thought like, "Is this a bug crawling on me that I have to get rid of?" or "Does this mean I'm developing a rash?"

In that sense, the itch is quite similar to a depressive thought that often feels very compelling, even though it may be transient. For example, if you have the thought that going to a social event will end in a disaster, you may act by staying home; you are in effect scratching that "itch" by avoiding a seemingly hazardous situation, because you believe your thought is a fact. But, like itches, thoughts do not mandate a specific action.

Viewing your emotions as if they were detached events like an itch or another body sensation like an ache can begin to change your relationship to them. Doing so can deplete them of their power to affect your mind's tendency to develop typical depressive stories. Moreover, it may diminish your feeling that you need to immediately try to gain relief. If you woke up with a neck ache one day in the past, you most likely did not feel compelled to take a specific action to relieve it. Viewing a depressive mood similarly as a mind/body symptom helps prevent blame and self-criticism; just as you wouldn't criticize yourself for the neck ache, so you don't need to criticize yourself for your thoughts. This doesn't mean there is not any pain, but the mindful approach allows the pain to be seen just as it is without elaboration.

Relinquishing the attempt to somehow fix yourself so you

never have an itch or a pain lifts a heavy burden. Developing the ability to tolerate such states without feeling compelled to fix them can be liberating. For example, when meditating you may become aware of yourself ruminating. "Ah! There I am ruminating again and that is part of my depression." Then you can actually have some power to decide if you want to continue the rumination or direct your attention elsewhere, such as back to your breath.

PART
II

Changing Your Relationship to Your Mind and Thoughts

YOUR MIND IS NOT ALWAYS YOUR FRIEND

The mind tends to do things it is particularly good at: thinking, problem solving, worrying, judging, and analyzing. But these things are often not in your best interest. It's somewhat like reading an article from a website or newspaper. What is written may not be accurate. If you suffer from depression, memories and thoughts tend to be biased toward the negative, which diminishes your problem-solving abilities. These factors may lead to misinterpretations, inaccurate assessments, and inappropriate decision making.

For example, Carol was walking down the street and saw a friend walking the other direction on the other side of the street. She waved to her but got no response. She felt rejected and depressed. Only later did she learn that her friend had been preoccupied by some bad news about a problem in her own life and hadn't noticed Carol. As she later learned, her friend was watching for an important business email she'd have to respond to.

Bill assessed himself as being incapable of completing a marathon. Only after joining a special training program did he realize he could be successful.

Sam thought of refusing a promotion, because he thought his

boss was setting him up to fail rather than having confidence in his ability to handle the new position. Such an approach could have severe consequences for his career.

A key step in coping with such thoughts is trying to decide if such situations are facts or just thoughts. Mindfulness gives you the space to look at the situation from multiple perspectives and without judgment. Then you can decide how to respond to the situation skillfully. You can evaluate your thoughts in several ways. One is to hold back on acting on a thought while you gather more data to assess whether the thought is a valid one. Another way of assessing a thought is to ask yourself how you feel in thinking it. If you feel more depressed (for example, "Yes, my friends really don't like me"), there is a very good chance the thought is being driven by depression.

One time, I was teaching a beginning class in meditation. One woman said, "I can't meditate as well as everybody else here." This is one of the most common thoughts of beginning meditators. Then several other members of the group expressed a similar idea about themselves. I asked them how they knew this, and as we assessed the situation, it became clear that such a thought was based more in the critical voice of depression rather than in any fact. Since none of the members had had any prior experience with meditation, it would be hard to expect anyone to be "better" than anybody else. Moreover, there actually is no competition in meditation; there is no score as in a game of basketball or golf. Mindful meditation is more about being present than about doing something better or worse than someone else.

So the woman's thought that she was somehow worse than others in her meditation practice was a valuable lesson about how her mind generated negative thoughts that were unnecessarily critical of her. She could begin to label them as such and become more able to bring her attention back to a neutral object like her breath. Perhaps just as important, when she was able to recognize such thoughts for what they were, she would not feel compelled to act on them by doing something such as dropping the class.

The Way Our Minds Work

The key element is that thoughts are not facts, even the ones that seem most compelling — perhaps the most compelling are even farther removed from the truth than other thoughts. If you can notice that your thoughts are just thoughts, passing mental events, they no longer hold compelling power over your responses.

The way the mind functions tends to remind me of a good friend I had growing up. Don was a great guy with a big heart who would do anything for a friend. However, his behavior exhibited a pattern of prevarication and exaggeration. Everyone in our circle of friends knew this pattern was part of his behavior. In fact, if someone said something that seemed unbelievable, we'd joke, "Who told you that? Don?" In many ways your mind is like Don. It has a lot of good features, but it prevaricates pretty regularly. It may not know it's prevaricating, but it is doing so nonetheless. In fact, the ideas it puts forth most definitively are the most likely to be false.

Take the example of Tom, who was getting angry at a colleague who didn't return an email. His mind was telling him quite strongly that he was being mistreated or rejected, but as we've seen, there are other options if you take a more mindful perspective. Perhaps the email had gone into a spam folder, and in that case no response occurred because the colleague had never viewed the email. Perhaps the colleague had been so overwhelmed by current life problems that she simply could not get to a response. Perhaps she just did not notice the email.

As Tom began to view the possibilities from a wider perspective, his emotions shifted dramatically. He realized that his thoughts about the email were just thoughts and that he really did not have much in the way of facts to shed light on his email experience. Although he had been so upset by the seeming lack of response that he considered cutting off all future communications with his colleague, he now realized that, had he continued to believe his initial thought, it could have ended disastrously. Instead, he reconnected with the person he had sent the email to and felt particularly good about doing so after he learned that she had been having trouble with her computer.

The skill you learn through mindfulness is to observe your mind without getting involved with it. We will talk more about the observing process in the next chapter, but for now, just try to recognize your mind as it thinks. Say, "Ah! There's my mind playing depression stories" or "Ah! There's my mind forecasting catastrophes." As you become proficient at observing these processes, don't expect that your mind will stop generating negative thoughts or feelings — minds tend to have their own biases, just like the news reports from certain television networks. You are just trying to change your relationship to your thoughts, to hold them more lightly. Remember, just because the thoughts are there doesn't mean you have to pay attention or be compelled to act because of them.

Sometimes our negative thoughts can be comforting, particularly because many of them are so familiar and often arose for the first time with important people in our lives. But if a thought produces an unpleasant sensation, it is most likely your mind not being your friend.

In one of the mindfulness classes we taught at UCSF, we were having a potluck to celebrate the end of the eight-week class. Before starting in on the treats, however, we had everyone lie on the floor on yoga mats, so we could do a body scan. One woman

The skill you learn through mindfulness is to observe your mind without getting involved with it.

illustrated the tendency of the mind's voice to generate critical thoughts. She described lying down for the body-scan meditation and noticed that she smelled something with a strong odor. Her first thought was, "I think my feet smell. Maybe this will disturb other people."

Then she went on to describe what happened next: "Before jumping onto the embarrassment train, I noticed I was lying near the table that had cheese on it that somebody had brought. Not accepting my first thought as a fact allowed me to realize that it was not my feet at all! The experience was the same — it was a smell, just a smell — but I labeled it initially as my smelly feet. When I obtained distance from that thought, I could perceive the truth of the situation."

Time Warp

The mind plays another trick in depression as well. It loses the perspective of time. For example, you might have the thought, "Will I be stuck in this depressive state forever?" You tend to forget the prior experiences of recovering from depression and think that you will remain in a depressive purgatory forever. It is easy to accept such a thought if you do not recognize it as just a thought. The mind tends to think that unpleasant states will go on forever and in fact projects that they will get worse with time. Of course, such a negative expectation, a depressive thought, tends to amplify the depressive state.

This type of expectation is common with pain of many types. People say, "I can't stand this" or "It will never get better." This applies to both physical pain and emotional pain, like the pain of depression and anxiety. Research[1] and my clinical experience show that actual pain values vary from expected pain values over a period of treatment. This is illustrated in the following graph I created.

Expected and Actual Pain Intensity

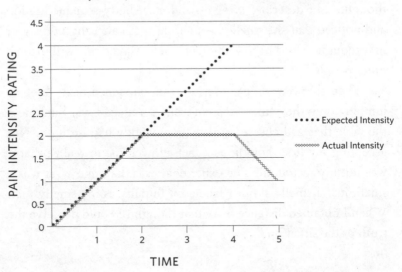

When you shine the spotlight of mindfulness on the pain, you find that the pain actually fluctuates even when it is at its worst level. Moreover, pain tends to level off or decrease with time and not indefinitely increase, as the graph indicates. The suffering associated with the pain can diminish even if the original stimulus does not. For example, people treated for panic disorder learn that, even though the panic attacks may continue, their response to them shifts. In this case the fear of panic attacks lessens.[2]

Your Mind Has Its Own Agenda

We see that the mind generates thoughts randomly, and when you're suffering from depression, the thoughts are typically negative. Your mind is not always your friend, and this applies especially to the thoughts you believe most strongly. If you are walking down the street and a stranger makes an insulting comment to you, it is easier to dismiss than if someone you care about makes the same comment.

In many instances the critical or negative thought that comes into awareness may have had its origins with important people from your past, for example, a critical parent. The beauty of the mindfulness-based cognitive approach is that whether you can actually identify who this person might be, you come to realize that the thoughts are merely mental events. They are not coming from an actual person in the present moment and do not have to be accepted as valid facts.

Remember Tom, who considered cutting off all communication with the colleague who didn't respond to his email? When he stepped out to view things from a wider perspective, he could see that there were other possible reasons for the nonresponse, and he was glad he did not act on his initial thought.

Here's the point. When your mind tells you to fix things in a certain way, such as by cutting off a relationship over an email, you do not immediately have to listen to it, no matter how stridently it shouts. Your observing self can be aware of the mind shouting its thoughts out. You can choose not to get involved in the stories the mind is generating about the email. Your mind may continue to voice its thoughts, but you can remove yourself to the position of the observing self, where you can watch the mind and react with equanimity. This position provides space to respond more skillfully. Assuming the position of the observer allows you freedom that you didn't have before.

Assuming the position of the observer allows you freedom that you didn't have before.

Rely on Your Observing Self

The observing self can help you see what is being generated by your mind and assess how you feel, both physically and emotionally. You then become capable of extending compassion to yourself and others.

Once when I was meditating during a body scan, my mind kept wandering to a situation at work where I had become agitated about an interaction with a colleague. My mind kept wanting me to replay this interaction, drawing me away from focusing on my breath and body parts. As I was experiencing this, I realized that my colleague was somebody I did not really care for. I thought to myself, "Why should I believe this voice?" Moreover, like the driver who cuts you off on the highway to take an exit, my colleague was undoubtedly *not* thinking about me. The whole agitation was my mind's creation. Once I had distance from this voice, I was able to let it go and bring my attention back to the body more easily.

The ruminative voices we hear are our constant source of distraction in depression, but they can shift as we alter our relationship to them. For example, one man had difficulties in his relationships with authority figures. He kept feeling he was being criticized or humiliated. As he gained more distance from such thoughts, however, he became able to view the thoughts as just thoughts. In fact, he said, "It's like I am seeing the same movie being replayed over and over." After he allowed the criticism/ humiliation tape to fade into the background, he began to have a different relationship with the authority figures in his life.

"The Guest House" was written by the Sufi poet Rumi around eight hundred years ago.[3] As you can see, the quest to manage our unpleasant moods and mental states has been going on for a long, long time. The normal human tendency is to avoid unpleasant experiences, but Rumi advocates a welcoming approach. Accepting such states instead of avoiding them may lead to greater flexibility in responding to situations. Your observing self can handle it.

THE GUEST HOUSE

This being human is a guest house.
Every morning a new arrival.

A joy, a depression, a meanness,
some momentary awareness comes
as an unexpected visitor.

Welcome and entertain them all!
Even if they are a crowd of sorrows,
who violently sweep your house
empty of its furniture,
still treat each guest honorably.
He may be clearing you out
for some new delight.

The dark thought, the shame, the malice,
meet them at the door laughing,
and invite them in.

Be grateful for whoever comes,
because each has been sent
as a guide from beyond.

If we expect that we can stop our minds from generating negative thoughts through meditation, we will be disappointed by our limitations. Our minds wander on their own, and our trying to control them makes them want to wander even more. In fact, experiments have shown that efforts to suppress thoughts actually intensify them. If you want to suppress a thought, you actually have to "push off" against the thought, and it intensifies the thought you are trying to suppress.

For example, Louise initially came to meditation practice to learn how to get her anxiety-inducing thoughts to cease. She soon realized that, although she wanted negative thoughts to stop completely, they never would. Instead, she learned in meditation that she did not have to pay much attention to them. The thoughts could be like the sounds of a radio that has the volume turned down, so it's a noise in the background, and they do not have to interfere with your functioning, goals, or values in life. When your mind generates negative thoughts, as all minds do, you now have the ability to relate differently to those thoughts. You will no longer have to latch on to depressive thoughts; rather, you can let them fade into the background.

Our minds are often not our friends in many everyday situations. Our minds are always trying to explain events. That is what our minds do and are built for: trying to organize and understand information. Humans have the need to try to conceptualize what is happening and to build hypotheses from an early age. For example, when an infant looks at patterns of black and white on a page, that's how they appear, as just black and white areas. Within a short time, however, the toddler becomes able to organize the black and white areas and recognize letters and words.

Similarly, we all organize events and pieces of information into stories we construct. This is often quite useful, but not always. When we do not understand something, we still try to organize it to fill in the blanks. We create stories, plots, and themes. In depression, this is often based on how we are feeling. Our emotional state can generate negative thoughts just as much as negative thoughts can generate a depressive state.

You can actually step back and observe yourself generating thoughts. Using the corn-popper analogy, you can monitor the kernels (thoughts) popping up in the next meditation.

TRY THIS: Observing Yourself Think

Close your eyes and focus on your breath for a minute or so.

Once your mind has steadied, take note of the thoughts that emerge over the next few minutes that tend to distract you from your breath. Ask yourself, "What is [fill in your name] thinking?" Notice what thoughts are emerging.

Ask again: "What is [fill in your name] thinking?" See what thoughts come up.

Then bring your attention back to the room.

The observing self was the self who was taking note of your thoughts. That self was watching you think, that is, watching your thoughts emerge. The observing self notices what you are thinking and feeling. Afterward, you might say, "I noticed my mind having a thought about [fill in the subject]." You might also say, "I noticed my mind producing depressive thoughts that then shifted my mood."

THOUGHTS ARE NOT FACTS

How to Befriend the Observing Self

I f your mind is constantly bubbling up negative ideas and stories, then who can you trust? This concept was beautifully illustrated by author Eckhart Tolle. In *The Power of Now*,[1] Tolle describes a low point in his life when he had suicidal ideas. He thought, "I cannot live with myself any longer." But then, in a moment of exceptional clarity, he realized that there were in fact two selves: his depressed self and a sense of presence, or "beingness," observing the depressed self. This realization brought about a marked sense of peace. This observing presence is the observing self, the one that notices what you are thinking or feeling.

The mind generates thoughts, judgments, analyses, feelings, and perceptions of the five senses. The observing self can view all of these. Remember my experiment with mindfulness techniques while I had a migraine? I started meditating and held the image of myself having a migraine: "There is Stu having a migraine." Shifting into that observer mode immediately reduced my suffering and the pain I was experiencing.

Someone in an MBCT group once labeled the observing self as a type of referee that looks down at what's happening. Another woman said that when she shifts to the observing self, she carries less anger and judgment around with her when interacting with others. She also found herself keeping score in her interactions far less often, because no scoring was indicated. So shifting from keeping score to not keeping score helped her feel better.

Assessing Negative Thoughts

In experimental studies individuals with depression are more likely to notice angry or sad faces than neutral or happy faces. Moreover, individuals with depression have a tendency to have difficulty recalling specific autobiographical memories except in a general and negative way. For example, they lump many different types of events in a "failures" category instead of seeing the individual differences and nuances between the events. In short, depressed individuals have a tendency toward the negative.

When your observing self becomes aware of negative thoughts, you are in position to assess them. Here are some examples of these thoughts:

I should be able to solve my problems by willpower.
Things will end up in a catastrophe.
It's terrible to show any weakness.
It's horrible if I ever feel sad.
I am a bad person.
I should never be angry with anyone.
I should never make mistakes.
He/she left me because I am worthless.

You will notice that these thoughts are judgments, evaluations, opinions — *not facts*. They are examples of jumping to negative conclusions and all-or-none thinking. They are negative thoughts based on some absolute standard that is difficult to achieve. These thoughts are strongly influenced by an inner critic.

When you are in the middle of a depressive state, it is easy to confuse such thoughts with facts. Decentering from these thoughts allows a mindful perspective that gives greater freedom in how you respond to these thoughts and the feelings associated with them.

Asking yourself whether what you are thinking is a thought or a fact is a concise tool for probing some of your firmly held beliefs, and you will often come up with surprising assessments. Bob had an experience when he was a teen in which a man had attempted to molest him. He had run away before any physical molestation had taken place, but he came away wondering why he had been targeted by the man. He felt ashamed, saw himself as a weakling, and questioned his own masculinity. He felt miserable and convinced that he was defective in some way. He went on to have a series of difficult relationships with authority figures because he felt inadequate.

Asking yourself whether what you are thinking is a thought or a fact is a concise tool for probing some of your firmly held beliefs.

When he took an MBCT class, he began to realize that his feeling of inadequacy was really a thought he was inadequate. He then began to challenge some of his thoughts. He recognized his beliefs about himself weren't necessarily true. Holding on to these beliefs kept him locked in disappointing situations. If he gave up the beliefs, he had the possibility of developing relationships that were more rewarding. In essence he realized that he had been operating under a delusion of inadequacy based on one traumatic episode. He eventually became able to view his incident with self-compassion and realize he had handled it as well as possible for a teenage boy.

In depression, a common belief is that you are inadequate, worthless, or deficient in some way. Which belief do you hold?

I'm sure you think that belief is true, but that's exactly what we're here to investigate. Ask yourself what evidence you have for the belief. Then ask yourself what good reason you have for continuing to hold the belief. The challenge here is that if you have been depressed for some time, you may have quite a bit of apparent evidence for your negative belief. Here is where decentering comes into play. Imagine your belief attached to a cloud passing through the sky. In this case the sky is your consciousness. Allow the cloud to drift through your sky until it disappears. Then notice how you feel. How does it feel to be without the belief, even momentarily?

When you engage your observing self, you can view your thoughts and emotions from a distance. This can help you understand that you are more than just someone having a specific disorder such as depression. In other words, the observing self allows more flexibility in how you see yourself.

Characteristics of the Observing Self

The observing self has a number of names in different philosophies and religions, such as the wise mind, the essential self, the Hindu Atman, or the Judeo-Christian soul. Buddhists have another way of conceptualizing the observing self's relationship to the mind. In Buddhism, people have six senses: feeling touches, smelling odors, seeing visions, tasting food, hearing sounds, and the thinking and feeling of the mind. For example, the mind generates thoughts, and it is the mind's nature to continuously do so, just as the other senses are constantly interacting with the environment.

In some ways, thoughts are like the lens through which we see the world. With mindfulness's observing capacity, you can see thoughts emerge just like the bubbles rising to the surface of a boiling pot. You can begin to notice that a wide range of thoughts come up to the surface of the pot and that you don't have to latch on to one in particular, but merely observe them as they come into being and then disappear.

Taking this perspective can give you a sense of new possibilities for the interactions and relationships in your life. Paradoxically, you can begin to have some sense of control, because you will be able to let go of thoughts that previously held sway and direct your attention where you would like to. You will be able to rewire your brain, so you do not remain locked in old patterns. Later in the book we will discuss some of the actual brain changes that occur.

Various forms of meditation may help illustrate the concept of an observing self. Jon Kabat-Zinn describes one meditation in which, in either a sitting or standing position, the individual takes on the bearing of a mountain. The individual imagines the seasons passing and various storms and elements of weather hitting the surface of the mountain. But the core of the mountain remains solid underneath, unfazed by what is happening on the surface. Similarly, our observing self can be seen as our own core. It remains solid, stable, and unmoving, perceiving but unaffected by the thoughts and feelings on its surface. It observes the mind's creations from a decentered perspective. With mindfulness, we do not deny that depression is present, but rather we view its effects from a solid, observing perspective.

Anna Swir's poem "Myself and My Person" beautifully illustrates the relationship between the observing self and your everyday self. She shows that even though you may have been listening to the self-critical voices of depression for a very long time, it is possible to turn to the observing self.

With mindfulness, we do not deny that depression is present, but rather we view its effects from a solid, observing perspective.

Myself and My Person

There are moments
when I feel more clearly than ever
that I am in the company
of my own person.
This comforts and reassures me,
this heartens me,
just as my tridimensional body
is heartened by my own authentic shadow.

There are moments
when I really feel more clearly than ever
that I am in the company
of my own person.

I stop
at a street corner to turn left
and I wonder what would happen
if my own person walked to the right.

Until now that has not happened
but it does not settle the question.

The observing mode is about shifting from a *doing* mode, in which you are trying to achieve success or specific accomplishment, into a *being* mode. Instead of trying to do or achieve something, in the being mode you are focused on being present in this moment and noticing whatever is there. Surprisingly, this may lead to actually accomplishing more than you would by concentrating all your efforts on achievement.

It is very common for individuals learning mindfulness to say, "I do not have enough time to practice mindfulness, because

I have so much to do." But mindfulness doesn't really require more time. For example, if you are eating, focusing on tasting your food doesn't require more time, although it means letting go of watching television at the same time. If you are walking, doing so mindfully means paying attention to the process, such as noticing the sensations in your feet and legs or your surrounding environment; you will get there in the same amount of time. Being mindful doesn't require more time, but rather more attention to what is happening in the present moment.

The object of the following meditation is not to walk a certain distance, but learning to focus on the sensations in your legs as you walk. Mindful walking, with its focus on the sensations occurring during the action, may be particularly useful as a way to shift out of depressive ruminations. Walking meditation is particularly useful when you are experiencing agitation or depression. Focusing on the body parts can have a dramatic calming effect and bring new awareness of how your lower limbs function.

TRY THIS: Walking Meditation

Select a comfortable setting at home where you can walk for fifteen or twenty feet without any obstructions.

From a standing position with feet evenly planted, begin by lifting the left foot into the air. Notice how the weight shifts to the right foot. Then, bringing the left foot down as you step forward, observe how the heel strikes the floor first and the sole of the foot progressively comes into contact with the floor.

Then begin to lift the right foot, noticing how the weight shifts to the left foot. Observe how the right foot leaves the floor: the right heel comes up, the right sole peels off the floor, and the toes help push off.

Continue walking slowly. A slower pace in the beginning will help you learn to identify your sensations, although you may feel a bit of unsteadiness because you are not used to walking slowly.

Close your eyes intermittently if you feel steady enough and comfortable doing so. Notice the sensations in your feet, ankles, lower legs, knees, upper legs, and hips as you walk.

As you are focusing on the sensations of the lower limbs, you may find your mind wandering to other sensations or thoughts — perhaps even thinking this is a silly meditation. When you notice such thoughts, congratulate yourself for noticing, then let them go, and return your focus to the limb sensations. That is the heart of mindfulness: intentionally focusing your awareness on the present moment and accepting it just as it is.

Continue your mindful walking for ten to fifteen minutes.

PART
III

Stumbling Blocks to Change and How to Overcome Them

ANXIETY

Depression's Frequent Partner

A nxiety is depression's bedfellow. They sleep in the same bed in the sense that they both derive their power from their relationship to time. When you suffer from depression, it feels as if a loss of some type has already occurred in your life and you typically feel bereft. If you are suffering from anxiety, you feel that a loss is going to take place at some point in the future and you approach that time with dread and fear. Anxiety often occurs in individuals who are suffering from depression as a co-occurring disorder. In our research, we found that of the individuals suffering from clinical depression 75 percent also suffered from an anxiety disorder. Perhaps you are experiencing an anxiety disorder alongside your depression.

TRY THIS: Observing Your Thoughts Using Your Finger

Close your eyes, and begin to observe your thoughts.

Using your right index finger as a meter, every time you have a thought about the future, move your finger to the right and then bring it back to the neutral center position. Every time you have a thought about the past, move it to the left and then again bring it back to the neutral position. When you have a thought about the present moment, leave your finger in the neutral position.

After you've observed your thoughts for a few minutes, open your eyes.

Were you surprised by how often your thoughts shifted away from the present moment? Just as significantly, did you notice how you can observe your thoughts arising and then passing away as the next one occurs? This capacity to observe your thoughts emerging in real time is a feature of your observing self. In this brief meditation you have an illustration of how many of your thoughts are linked to the past and depressive themes and how many are linked to the future and anxious possibilities.

Oftentimes it may be hard for you to tell whether anxiety or depression comes first. In fact, Myrna Weissman and colleagues investigated the family tree of individuals whose parents and grandparents had both had depression. These individuals were genetically predisposed toward depression. When the investigators looked at the third generation, they found that the first symptoms to emerge were of anxiety, not depression. Only several years later did clinical depression become evident.[1] We now know that many of the same areas in the brain that are hyperactive in depression are also hyperactive in anxiety states, so there is significant overlap between the two conditions. Even though they share certain features, their observable appearance is often considerably different.

Anxiety Disorders

Anxiety ailments can take many forms: panic disorder, social anxiety disorder, generalized anxiety disorder, and specific phobias. Although no longer classified formally as anxiety disorders, post-traumatic stress and obsessive-compulsive disorders also share features of anxiety. Let's look briefly at each one.

Panic disorder begins with panic attacks. Panic attacks are limited-time episodes in which you experience heart palpitations, sweating, shortness of breath, chest pain, gastrointestinal symptoms, and a fear of dying or losing your mind. In fact, for 40 percent of individuals coming to the emergency room for chest pain, a panic attack is the cause of their symptoms. Panic attacks reach the level of a disorder when you begin to be so worried about having another panic attack that you start to avoid situations out of fear.

Kathy started having panic attacks when she was eighteen years old and going away to college for the first time. At first they were intermittent, but they became progressively more troubling for her. She suffered a racing heart, sweating, flushing, and dizziness. She initially went to the emergency room for what she feared was a heart attack. After an evaluation, she was told that her heart was fine. She was suffering a panic attack. She then began to avoid situations in which her panic attacks had occurred, such as in a crowd and sometimes in a classroom. The number of the situations gradually grew, and her fear of having another episode severely limited her activity and threatened her college experience.

Kathy came in for an MBCT class after a friend recommended it. She began learning more about the sensations she experienced by doing the body scan. As the class progressed, she began to notice her thoughts. She was surprised by how much her thinking focused on future catastrophes. After she began to notice these thoughts, she realized how much negative "propaganda" she was bombarding herself with.

She gradually realized that the thoughts were just that — thoughts, and not necessarily accurate predictions about the future. As this process unfolded, she began to see her panic attacks as unpleasant events but not disasters. For example, when she had a thought of a looming disaster, she would ask herself, "Is that a thought or a fact?" She also began to see that her disaster scenarios were like a familiar movie that she had already seen and not a foregone reality. She became more comfortable going to the places she had avoided, even if she were to risk a panic attack.

> When she had a thought of a looming disaster, she would ask herself, "Is that a thought or a fact?"

Social anxiety disorder is another type of anxiety condition in which the fear of embarrassment or humiliation in social situations takes prominence. For example, Joe turned down a promotion at work because it required him to give presentations to various groups. His fear of appearing stupid in front of others severely limited his potential career options and made him tense during much of the day. Individuals with social anxiety disorder often set unrealistically high standards for themselves and berate themselves when they fall short.

Worry about the future is a central feature of *generalized anxiety disorder*. Such pervasive worry crowds out the ability to be focused on the present moment and to take any enjoyment in life. The worry may appear to you as if you are appropriately anticipating some disaster that will happen in the future. But as time goes on, the worry precludes normal emotional processing.

Angela came to treatment hoping to get rid of her anxious thoughts. She had worried since childhood about one problem or another continuously. She was married and had a family of three teenagers. She worried that something bad was going to happen to them. She worried about accidents, illnesses, and a variety of other potential disasters. If her son was late coming home from an event, she was certain something terrible had happened, such as a car accident. She was continually anxious, and this was getting worse as her children began to increasingly be away from home.

She started attending MBCT classes and developed a mindfulness practice. She began to notice where in her body her anxiety was most evident. She noticed that her abdomen felt tight and constricted and her breathing felt shallow. She began to see that her thoughts, particularly her anxious ones, were just thoughts and she did not have to believe they were true.

Angela utilized the meditation of seeing her thoughts as the cars of a freight train. She could picture herself on a bridge looking down at her thoughts as the train passed by. She could watch the thoughts fade into the distance without jumping on the train herself. As she continued her practice, she came to see her worrying thoughts moving off into the distance like the cars of the train. With time, she began to think of her thoughts as if they were music playing in the background. She came to see that, instead of trying to stop all her worrying thoughts, she could go about her life even though the music was playing.

Specific *phobias* include fear of such things as flying, bridges, heights, or insects. The sufferer persistently avoids a specific object, activity, or situation. For example, agoraphobia is the fear of being in a place, such as a crowded shopping center, in which escape may be difficult. This can occur as an isolated disorder, but also often occurs commonly in conjunction with panic disorder.

Ron, thirty-four years old, came in for treatment of symptoms of panic disorder and a phobia connected with travel. He had developed panic attacks shortly after his son was born. The attacks occurred whenever he had to travel out of town on short business trips. Usually the attacks occurred when he had to drive across a bridge or travel on the highway. His fears about the attacks began to seriously affect his ability to do the travel his job required. Ron also began to experience rapid heart rate along with chest pain and tingling fingers when he went away on these trips. This brought him to the emergency room on several occasions. Several thorough cardiac evaluations, however, came back normal.

He came to our clinic for treatment after his primary-care physician suggested that mindfulness might be helpful for his panic disorder. He described his persistent worry about his wife's ability to manage their newborn when he left home on his trips, despite the fact that his wife was a pediatric nurse practitioner who also had the help of her nearby mother.

Ron initially was skeptical about mindfulness, but found the meditations relaxing. Soon he began to have a different perspective on his panic attacks. He could see them as symptoms that did not actually lead to a disaster. In fact, he experimented with trying to produce the panic symptoms by spinning himself around in an office chair. This rapid type of movement had precipitated panic attacks in the past. When he tried doing this now, he could see the panic symptoms arise and then fade away. His attitude about panic attacks shifted, because what used to feel like a looming heart attack had been reduced to an unpleasant set of sensations that he could tolerate. As he came to feel more in control of his own life, he felt more confident about his wife's mothering skills and was less worried when he went on his trips.

Avoidance Is Not the Answer

Any anxiety disorder can lead to depression. For example, if Joe were to keep turning down possible promotions at work because he was afraid of a social situation, he would end up in a very limited position. He could become depressed over the situation, especially when he saw his peers making progress in their careers. If you are experiencing depression that you think is anxiety-based, addressing the depression is important, but it's also critical that you find a way to approach the situation you've been avoiding.

This is often not easy, because you've probably learned through experience that avoidance reduces your anxiety over the short term. For example, avoiding public speaking may diminish anxiety about that type of situation, but would be likely to lead to depression if your life goal was to be a teacher, who needs to be able to speak in front of the class.

The key point, however, is that avoidance only works on a temporary basis. In other words, if you avoid the feared situation, you will temporarily reduce anxiety, but eventually such avoidance tends to restrict your activity and freedom. So the more you avoid, the greater the impact the feared situations have on you.

Mindfulness can help you realize that your thoughts about the situation are merely mental events. In some respects, your depressive thought patterns are more like a disaster movie than a disaster newsreel. They are a fantasy, whereas the newsreel is a reasonably accurate depiction of reality. With anxiety disorders, there is typically a blurring of the distinction between these two modes. Mindfulness helps you become more aware of which type of film is running through your head.

In some instances, people find that it's not the anxious thoughts that are most troubling; it's the inner critical voice about having the thoughts. This issue was illustrated by one middle-aged woman who came to our MBCT class. Maria entered treatment for lifelong anxiety. She had accomplished quite a bit in her life; she was a successful businesswoman and wife. Yet she chronically felt "the other shoe was going to drop." This feeling applied to new developments in her work as well as concerns about her family. Her sister had suffered similar worries and had benefited from a mindfulness approach, so Maria was willing to give it a try.

She initially complained only about the anxious thoughts she was experiencing. But as time went on, she began to notice she had a voice in her mind that was persistently critical. This inner critic told her that she shouldn't be feeling the way she did or that something was wrong with her for thinking such anxious thoughts. As her mindfulness practice strengthened, she began to see her thoughts and feelings as mental events that did not require critical judgment. She began to notice where in her body her anxiety rested. She noticed tightness in her chest and felt her lungs weren't fully expanding with her breath. She could observe her thoughts emerging periodically from a distance and treat them with a sense of humor as well. She did not have to believe the thoughts were true.

As her practice continued, she became progressively more comfortable accepting her thoughts and sensations just as they were without trying to change them. She was able to stay more in the present moment and relinquish her concerns about the future. Her thoughts and feelings continued, but her attitude toward them changed. Instead of being self-critical, she began to feel compassion toward herself for suffering such worries. Importantly, they did not mean that she was a weak or deficient person. They were just thoughts and feelings.

As these stories illustrate, when individuals come in for treatment, they are understandably trying to get rid of their anxious thoughts. In the mindfulness approach, however, the focus is not on getting rid of the thoughts, but rather changing one's relationship to them. For example, when treating someone with panic disorder, a therapist might actually try to induce the panic attack by having the person revisit the trigger, as Ron did by spinning himself in the chair. In this way, the individual has the opportunity to learn that what is being experienced is only a panic attack and not the imagined catastrophe. In mindfulness, the focus is on helping the person to accept the panic sensations and thoughts as transient mental events.

In the radio analogy, patients come in wanting to turn off the radio completely, but soon discover that they can change their relationship to the sounds. Someone experiencing anxiety doesn't have to believe everything the radio is playing or accept it as valid. The thoughts, the noisy sounds coming from the radio, are not accurate predictions of future events; they are background noise. Even with the radio playing, you can still move forward in your life.

Steven C. Hayes, the founder of acceptance and commitment therapy (ACT), described his own experience with panic disorder in a lecture he gave at the University of California at San Francisco. He was a young psychologist at a university when he began suffering panic attacks. He became progressively more confined. He began spending more time at home and participating less in university life, including teaching activities.

What drew him out of confinement was an awareness that he really wanted to be a productive teacher and recognized as a valuable member of the teaching faculty. Instead of staying at home, he began returning to his teaching endeavors despite his panicky sensations. Courage is not acting without fear, but rather despite fear. His values and goals helped him resume functioning. His perspective shifted away from seeing his panic attacks as a prison and toward the idea that they were something he could live with even if he wasn't able to turn the radio off.

> *Courage is not acting without fear, but rather despite fear.*

False Evidence

All anxiety disorders are rooted in the human survival feature of being on guard against potential threats. Fear is an adaptive response to a realistic threat. It prepares you to take action. If a lion is standing in front of you, fear is an appropriate response and may be quite useful in your survival. With anxiety disorders, the perceptions that occur are quite similar, although they may be summarized as false evidence.

For example, while talking in a group session, Katie thought people weren't interested in what she was saying and felt embarrassed about her remarks. When other group members commented, however, it was clear that they valued her opinion and that her embarrassment was due to false evidence. In fact, when you notice distressing thoughts, asking yourself "Are they false evidence?" is a good yardstick to hold your thoughts up to. Questioning the validity of the evidence may give you a new perspective on your situation.

The Trier Social Stress Test, which was originally devised to measure physiological stress indicators, illustrates the mechanism at work here. In this test, an individual gives a brief talk on a topic of his or her own choosing. The stress comes from having a small audience purposely fail to pay attention to the talk. This is typically quite unsettling, producing a flood of negative thoughts and elevated stress hormones. But individuals can be trained to ignore the audience response and reduce their stress levels. In the case of the test, the audience inattention was planned and real. But for people with anxiety or depression it is often the illness that creates the "inattention" — as in Katie's case — and it is common for them to jump to a negative conclusion based on false evidence.

Mindfulness helps you develop some distance between an event and your response, so that instead of reacting reflexively to the situation, you can respond skillfully. Psychologist Rian McMullin gives a graphic illustration of this point. Aging lions tend to lose their teeth, but they still participate in hunting with their pride. They do so by roaring and driving prey toward the younger lions, which still possess their teeth. If the prey were aware of the situation, they would actually be better off running toward the roar, not away from it.[2] Running toward the roar is a key to reducing the impact of anxiety in your life.

With anxiety, like depression, certain areas of the brain are altered from their normal state. The systems in the brain that regulate emotions are in some respects taken offline so that the emotional responses are predominant. For example, the amygdala is a section of the brain that is involved with filtering or amplifying different stimuli. With anxiety and depression, this area is hyperactive, leading to heightened fear responses. For example, in fMRI studies of individuals with anxiety and depression, viewing neutral faces tended to produce responses similar to viewing negative faces like angry ones. On the other hand, brain areas that dampen emotional reactivity like the dorsolateral prefrontal cortex are decreased in depression and anxiety.

Mindfulness practice has been shown to reverse these changes, bringing the prefrontal cortex back toward normal and diminishing the activation of the amygdala. In other words, mindfulness has real effects on normalizing brain function. Thanks to a quality of the brain called neuroplasticity (which we will discuss in Appendix B), you can actually use mindfulness practices to change how your brain functions.

Fear is a normal human emotion, but when your fears are based on false stimuli, we can label the response as anxiety. This becomes a disorder when you try to avoid the stimuli, sometimes at all costs. For example, staying in your room to avoid an object or situation restricts your life. The path to healing does not lie in avoidance, but rather in approaching the situation or object that triggers your fear. Only then will

The path to healing does not lie in avoidance, but rather in approaching the situation or object that triggers your fear. Only then will you learn that it doesn't have the destructive power you believed it did.

you learn that it doesn't have the destructive power you believed it did.

Jennifer Paine Welwood's beautiful poem "Unconditional" illustrates these points.

UNCONDITIONAL

Willing to experience aloneness,
I discover connection everywhere;
Turning to face my fear,
I meet the warrior who lives within;
Opening to my loss,
I gain the embrace of the universe;
Surrendering into emptiness,
I find fullness without end.
Each condition I flee from pursues me,
Each condition I welcome transforms me
And becomes itself transformed
Into its radiant jewel-like essence.
I bow to the one who has made it so,
Who has crafted this Master Game;
To play it is purest delight —
To honor its form, true devotion.

ANGER AND ITS IMPACT
ON DEPRESSION

Anger can be a powerful driver of depression. For example, feeling helpless about a situation can produce anger. The anger may then be transformed into a depressive state. Anger's relationship to depression may also be bidirectional. For example, when you are depressed, it feels as if a loss of some type has already taken place. This sense of loss may lead to irritability and anger, but when depressed, you may not feel entitled to express your feelings. Anger may sometimes be related to feeling hurt in some way. In some instances, it may not be apparent what you are angry about, but some investigation may clarify things.

Susan was a sixty-one-year-old woman who had been evaluated by a neurologist for a marked tremor of the right hand. She was very depressed, because no one had been able to help her. The evaluation had revealed no organic etiology, and she was referred for psychiatric treatment. When she came to treatment with me, she explained that the tremor had started after her husband had suffered a severe heart attack and undergone coronary artery bypass surgery. As a result of his illness, the couple had to cancel the around-the-world cruise that they had been planning for years as part of their retirement celebration. She denied any feelings of disappointment about being unable to go on the planned cruise.

When I asked Susan what kind of motion her hand was making as it shook, she replied, "A spanking motion." As we examined this further, I asked if she might have some angry feelings about being unable to go on the long-planned and long-anticipated cruise. She replied that she couldn't be angry, "because it was not his fault." I pointed out that even though that was true, anger wasn't always particular about its target. Furthermore, anger was not an all-or-nothing emotion — she could still love him and not blame him *and* feel a little angry.

When she stepped into an observing-self mode, she could see that she did feel some anger about the disappointment. At the same time, she recognized that her husband's illness had not been aimed at her. When she was able to observe in this way, her anger diminished, her depression abated, and her spanking tremor disappeared. Of course, not every instance of depression combined with anger is going to have such a clear-cut connection. The point here is that striving to investigate the relationship between anger and depression can often be beneficial.

In other cases, it's not that anger is unrecognized. On the contrary, it is acknowledged and out in the open — you know you're mad. The problem comes with the way you choose to interpret the cause of that anger. Take the example we used earlier of driving down the interstate in the middle lane. A car from the far-left lane suddenly cuts across in front of you and exits to the right. You have to jam on your brakes a bit, but no damage occurs. Understandably you might be angry at the other driver. This could affect your mood, sometimes for a considerable period of the day if you replay the event in your mind. If you take it as a personally aimed action, you might get really upset.

George described such an event and said he thought that the person cut him off because George was shorter than average, that the other person was specifically picking on him because of his height. Even though this idea seems preposterous to an outside observer, for George the idea led him to feel quite angry. George's feeling stuck in this situation, with no way to act on his feelings, led him to become depressed at this latest episode of perceived mistreatment.

George's reaction needs more exploration. In the first place, George's anger did not do him much good in rectifying the situation, as the other driver had driven off and had little if any awareness of George's experience. Moreover, had George viewed the situation more mindfully, he might have changed his perspective and not reacted so reflexively. Perhaps the other driver was ill or driving a pregnant spouse to the hospital; perhaps the other driver was not very skilled or not very respectful of others.

We can be almost certain that the action was not aimed at George and certainly not because he was short. With a more mindful perspective, he could have responded without the emotional uproar, which also had lingering effects on his mood. Instead, he remained locked in a ruminative cycle, which just wasted energy and made him feel worse.

Your Own Anger

What do you know about your own anger? Mindfulness allows you to utilize the gap between the impulse and action and offers you the freedom to act skillfully rather than reflexively.

TRY THIS: Observing Your Anger

When you are feeling anger, go to a quiet space, close your eyes, and watch the thoughts that arise from it. Your anger is a burner causing thought bubbles to rise to the surface of your mind; the anger is in essence powering the thoughts.

Observe those thoughts and decenter from them. You are not your anger — you do not have to be fused with it or the bubbles coming up; rather, you can just observe them.

Use the lens of self-compassion to help you see that millions of people are experiencing anger just as you are.

Observe your anger just as if you were holding an object in your hand. Study it. Learn its details, its nooks and crannies, and the kind of thoughts it produces. See that the thoughts flowing from the anger are just thoughts, not facts.

Let the anger "cook" until all the rawness is processed, so you can respond skillfully.

Floating Logs

Anger typically arises when you think things should be other than the way they are and that someone has specifically aimed the situation at you. A classic Tao story is about a floating log. A fisherman anchors his boat on the river for the night. He goes down into his cabin to settle in for sleep. Suddenly he hears a sound like another boat hitting his. In a fury, he rushes up the steps to the deck, angry at whoever may have damaged his boat. Once he gets to the deck, he sees that it was a floating log that hit his boat. It had simply drifted into his boat.

> Anger typically arises when you think things should be other than the way they are and that someone has specifically aimed the situation at you.

What happens to his anger? As soon as he sees that it was a log, much if not all of the anger dissipates and subsides. He can see that the collision was not something aimed at him. He will still have to deal with whatever damage was done, but there's no one specific to blame.

In the same way, much of what happens in life is in actuality a similar floating-log collision. There may be damage, but it is usually not aimed at us specifically. We are all hit by floating logs at times. The consequences may still be unpleasant, but the fury of ideas that surrounded the incident when you were "below deck" can now drift away.

One incident brought many of these points home for me. I had gone to the post office to mail a package. When I arrived, there was just one woman in line in front of me. The woman turned to me and said she came to this post office frequently and that one of the two clerks was very slow. The other clerk was occupied with a customer who had about thirty packages that she was sealing individually and then handing to the clerk one by one. Shortly the line began to grow. I could hear the fellow behind me getting irate with the customer at the counter for not sealing her packages ahead of time. I began to feel some anger about the situation too, but I was able to shift to a more mindful perspective.

In the first place, the behavior was clearly not aimed at me. Second, I had a choice about how to respond. I could become irate, or I could choose to accept the situation as it was. It would only delay me a few minutes. I decided that a brief breathing meditation might be helpful, so I began counting my breaths. Focusing on the breath by counting helps us become aware of thoughts flowing through our consciousness. Which would be more beneficial: responding angrily or mindfully? The choice was clear. More important, I realized (once again) that I had a choice. I did not have to react reflexively.

In another example relating to anger, an MBCT group member gave his teenage son permission to go to an event that would not be over until 11 PM. He gave his son explicit instructions to be home by 11:30. As the clock ticked past that time, the father felt himself growing angrier with each minute. Because we had discussed how to deescalate and he'd done some practicing, he took a few breaths and tried to observe what was happening. He could feel the tightness in his muscles.

As he mindfully noticed how angry he was, he was able to view it with some distance. He became aware that the anger that he was feeling was really a response to the fear he felt that his son might have been involved in some type of accident. When the son came home at midnight, instead of berating him, the father explained that he had felt very worried about him and asked how the situation could be prevented in the future. This opened up a useful dialogue with the son rather than an angry exchange.

Depression as Unexpressed Anger

Depression is often a clue that anger is not being expressed. Wendy was upset that her boyfriend did not want to move forward with having a child, and she became depressed. The mood was a clue that she was angry about something, but wasn't expressing it to the person she felt angry at. One way of understanding the relationship between anger and depression is to ask yourself, "Who am I depressed at?"

One way of understanding the relationship between anger and depression is to ask yourself, "Who am I depressed at?"

After Wendy began her mindfulness practice, she began to widen her perspective on her boyfriend's stance. She originally thought it was aimed at her and was some type of personal rejection. As she listened more closely to his comments about the situation, she realized that he had many concerns about what type of father he would be and that his fears about this were the primary motivator for his position. It had much less to do with his feelings about her. With this realization, she was able to let her anger subside and have a more meaningful discussion with him about the idea of parenting.

Suppressing angry feelings, often done willingly because a person fears disrupting a relationship, can itself cause depression. This happened for Ellen, who had moved to San Francisco with her husband of twenty-five years, because he had a terrific job opportunity there. Ellen, however, had given up very gratifying work at a nonprofit organization she was passionate about and thought she would have a difficult time replicating it in a new city. She had a difficult time acknowledging, or even being aware of, the anger she felt about the situation, because this was such a wonderful opportunity for her husband. How could she be angry about that?

She gradually began to notice that angry feelings would leak out sometimes. As her mindfulness practice increased, she became aware of her choice to be angry about the situation or respond more skillfully. She began deepening her exploration of possibilities in her new city and found a position that she really enjoyed that had many of the satisfying qualities of her prior work.

And then there was John. He suffered from severe depression that had withstood the full spectrum of medications and electroconvulsive treatment. He voiced a belief that his illness was purely biological. He was waiting for the right treatment to help him. Though he was not at all optimistic, he was referred for mindfulness-based cognitive therapy as something that could potentially be helpful for him.

When we first met, he vehemently resisted the idea that there were any psychological factors involved in his depression. After we talked for a while, he mentioned that his depressive episode had developed when his daughter and wife had gone abroad on a vacation without him. He said he had no feelings about this, since he could not have gone due to his work schedule and he did not want to deny his wife and daughter a bonding experience. He also revealed that he had been abandoned by his father early in life and forced to work to support his entire family throughout his life. Because of his cultural heritage and character, he saw no alternative and could not overtly express any anger or resentment about his wife and daughter leaving on their trip.

With mindfulness he gradually became aware that he could hold feelings both positive (such as wanting his wife and daughter to have a wonderful time) and negative (such as feeling abandoned) at the same time. He also learned that if an angry feeling occurred, it was permissible to allow it to exist without having to act upon it or inflict some damage as a result. With this approach his depressive symptoms decreased significantly, though it took some time. He ended his mindfulness class by signing up for an MBCT alumni group.

By observing your thoughts, you can gain perspective on them rather than being fused with them and at their mercy; you can respond rather than react. You can train yourself to become a better observer through your mindfulness practice.

TRY THIS: Watching Your Thoughts Come and Go

Begin by focusing on the breath, and allow yourself to steady your concentration. With your eyes closed, focus on the breath as it moves in and out of the nostrils; feel the air currents moving in and out. Perhaps you can notice turbulence in the air currents at the tip of the nose. Perhaps you can feel the temperature variation between the air flowing in through the nostrils and the air moving out.

Now imagine yourself as a well-fed outstretched cat silently watching a mouse hole directly in front of you. The cat is your observing self, and the mice are your thoughts. As you lie in wait, perhaps no thought emerges right away. But as you continue to wait, you notice a thought emerging out of the mouse hole. Watch the thought scamper away, and then gently return your gaze to the mouse hole to await the next thought.

As your observing self, watch the thoughts as they come and go without getting caught up in trying to capture one. Practice this technique for five minutes.

You may notice as you carry out this meditation that your attention tends to wander at times, or perhaps most of the time. If so, congratulate yourself for noticing the wandering — that is a key step in being mindful.

PART
IV

Lasting Ways
to Achieve Happiness

COMPASSION AND SELF-COMPASSION

Antidotes for Anger and Allies in Combating Depression

Mindfulness helps individuals focus on the present moment, diminishing rumination about the past and the imagination of catastrophes in the future. Mindfulness also helps people to become gentler and more compassionate with themselves. As one fellow said, "If I can forgive myself for my mind wandering, I can begin to forgive myself for other things too." In some studies of the mechanisms of mindfulness, self-compassion appears to be one of the most important ingredients in producing change.[1]

Choosing Compassion

As the previous chapter indicates, being able to identify anger is particularly beneficial, because it allows you to become more skillful in responding to it. Some time ago, I was at a silent retreat lasting seven days. The purpose of the retreat was to apply mindfulness throughout the day for all activities ranging from specific meditation sessions to things such as eating meals. The big meal of the day was lunch, and one day I was really looking forward to eating that meal mindfully in the dining hall. I got my food, sat down, and began my attempt to eat mindfully, closing my eyes and trying to really taste the food. Then a man came, sat down across from me, and started a series of sniffling noises that he kept up several times per minute.

I started to become very irritated. Why did this guy have to sit here and not somewhere else? Why did he have to interfere with my eating meditation? This was the high point of the day, and he was ruining it for me. I fantasized about throwing a napkin at him, and then I remembered one of the important teachings about anger. Buddhist monk and philosopher Matthieu Ricard teaches that the antidote for anger is compassion.[2] I thought I would try a bit of compassion here and apply it to this fellow.

I said to myself, "Maybe this poor guy has a cold or allergies or some other illness going on." Remembering the floating-log story, I knew he was certainly not doing this *to me*. He was just doing it. I do not think he sat down and said, "Let me see if I can interfere with somebody's eating meditation." So, once I started to feel some compassion for him, almost magically my anger dissipated, and I could return to my eating meditation without interruption.

This had another application. If I could apply compassion to someone else, why not apply it to myself? I feel angry with myself on a regular basis, so perhaps I could take another lesson from this incident and apply compassion to myself as well.

The observing self is capable of extending compassion toward yourself as well as others. It is like a caring person from your past who was kind and gentle. You might imagine this loving figure as always available to help guide your perspective on the material your mind is generating.

During that same retreat, I was in a meditation hall where the door creaked and squeaked every time it was opened by latecomers entering the hall after the meditation session had started. I asked the retreat manager if it could be corrected, but that had little effect on the situation. I began to get angry at the conditions of the hall that were interfering with my meditation. Then I tried taking a more mindful approach. I thought about the birds outside the hall that would noisily take flight from a tree following a flock leader and then just as noisily return to the same tree, taking off and returning every few minutes. "Why are the birds doing that?" I wondered.

I decided to think of the people coming into the hall as birds, noisily coming back to the same tree time and time again. I had not been upset about the bird noise; it was obviously not aimed at me. Why should I be angry at the latecomers? I could have compassion for them too. They arrived late for one reason or another, but not to punish me! After I shifted my perspective like this, my anger disappeared.

Conversely, when I came in, causing the door to creak, and someone appeared visibly upset with me, that was a good clue that that person was taking the situation personally. But I could be compassionate with myself — I was like the birds coming back to roost.

Another opportunity to extend compassion and not take things personally came up in one of our MBCT groups. Mary Ann initially signed up to be in the group, but shortly before the first session she called to cancel, saying it was too far for her to come. Then she called back saying she wanted to give it a try. During the first few sessions she was quite negative about the group's supposed shortcomings, although there was little apparent evidence for her opinion, since she had never experienced any mindfulness training. Then she decided to drop out, saying it wasn't for her. Two weeks later she called and said she wanted to finish the class.

I was irritated with her and somewhat angry about her marked ambivalence, and I considered refusing her request to rejoin. Then I thought about the situation with more compassion. Compassion means to travel with others who are suffering. Her ambivalence was not aimed at me or even the class; it was a result of her psychological issues. I allowed her to rejoin the group, and she became a strong and enthusiastic participant. She revealed extensive marital turmoil related to her husband's loss of his job and her fears about being destitute. In the final three sessions of the class, she began to see her situation from different viewpoints, and her depression lessened considerably.

When you suffer from depression, it is important to extend compassion to yourself. This means being able to be kind to yourself and treat yourself with gentleness. With depression, however, your capacity to do so is often reduced. Indeed, most people who suffer from depression have a particularly harsh inner critic. This critic can be noisy when you make a mistake or fail but can even find the negative when you succeed, chalking it up, for example, to luck. Self-compassion is an antidote for the inner critic.

Compassion means to travel with others who are suffering.

The RAIN Technique

The RAIN technique for working with emotions was originally developed by meditation teacher Michele McDonald to allow for engagement with the present moment. Other teachers, such as Tara Brach, have incorporated the technique into their work because of its broad utility in dealing with difficult emotions. I teach this four-step method to people dealing with anger.

TRY THIS: The RAIN Technique

RAIN stands for Recognize, Accept, Investigate, and Nonidentify.

Recognize when a strong emotion is present: "I'm feeling angry."

Accept the presence of the emotion. In this case, accept that you are experiencing anger. Try to do so in an open and nonjudgmental way.

Investigate the thoughts, feelings, and sensations that are present. What thoughts go through your mind? Do you think that you are being treated unfairly? Is someone specifically aiming something harmful toward you? What feelings are you aware of? Anger, guilt, shame, embarrassment? Where in your body do you feel the anger? Is there a constriction in the chest or abdomen? Is the breath more rapid? Are the muscles tense? Should you act on your angry feelings or is there another response you could make?

Nonidentification with the emotion. Shift into the observing-self mode — "Ah, there's me feeling angry" — putting distance between yourself and the angry feelings. See the anger as a mental event separate from you. You are not your angry feelings. Just as thoughts come into awareness, so do feelings. They are like clouds drifting across the sky. Some may be light, while others are dark and foreboding. But they all pass through your consciousness, which remains a constant. Rather than looking at your thoughts and feelings from *within* them, stand *outside* of them and view them dispassionately, without judgment or criticism.

How Self-Compassion Counters Depression

According to leading researcher Kristin Neff, there are three elements of self-compassion that contrast to aspects of depression.[3] The first is *self-kindness*, which stands in opposition to *self-criticism*, that disparaging voice that is common in depression. The second is a sense of *common humanity*, an awareness that others share the same suffering. The contrasting element in depression is a sense of *isolation and shame*; the tendency to isolate or insulate oneself from social contacts is often related to a sense of shame over feeling inadequate.

The third element is *mindfulness* and the ability to view one's thoughts and feelings from some distance instead of overidentifying with them. *Overidentification* is the tendency to accept negative aspects of oneself as proven facts. For example, I am overidentifying when I think I am a bad person and accept that judgment as true, but mindful when I see it as just another thought that may or may not be a fact. Overidentification with the negative is a common symptom of depression.

Our research indicated that people completing our training had increased self-compassion as well as decreased depression levels. This was consistent with research by Neff and others who found that enhanced self-compassion is associated with reduced anxiety, depression, and stress. An attitude of self-kindness softens the self-criticism of depression.

Practicing Self-Compassion

Let me explain how to practice self-compassion. Let's say you make a mistake on a project you have been working on. Your inner critic might say something like, "How stupid of me" or "How incompetent." Applying the lens of self-compassion sets a different tone: "That was a difficult problem; many people might have made that mistake. I know how to correct the mistake now."

Self-compassion is built upon appreciating the common humanity of your situation. Humans make errors; mistakes are part of what we all experience throughout our lives. In fact, our ties to others are bound more by our *imperfections* than our perfections.

> *Self-compassion is built upon appreciating the common humanity of your situation. Humans make errors; mistakes are part of what we all experience throughout our lives.*

This simple meditation can have a remarkable effect in demonstrating your connections with others.

TRY THIS: Common Humanity

Practice "Just like me." As you go through your daily life, observe other people who cross your path, and practice seeing them as fellow travelers, with you, on the road of life. For example, when you are at a stoplight, look over at the driver next to you and say:

Just like me, they want to be happy.
Just like me, they make mistakes and suffer too.
Just like me, they are doing their best in the world.

With self-compassion and common humanity in mind, you might also say to yourself, "I made a mistake. That's what humans do." You can choose to avoid berating yourself. This means if you notice yourself starting to criticize yourself, you can mindfully recognize what is occurring and then choose to focus on the event with self-compassion. Sometimes people worry that dampening the self-critical voice will lower their standards. However, people who have reasonable levels of self-compassion do not lower their standards. Instead, they are not devastated if they don't meet them. As a consequence, they are more willing to try new or challenging things, because they don't see failure as disaster.

A highly successful businessman was once interviewed by a journalist. The interviewer asked the businessman how he had become so successful. He replied, "Good decisions." The interviewer then asked how he had gotten such good decision-making ability. The businessman replied, "Good experience." The interviewer then asked how he had obtained such good experience. The businessman replied, "Bad decisions."

The Inner Critic

The balance between the inner critic and self-compassion is evident in many settings. Although there's value in having an inner critic to correct behavior, usually in depression the inner critic is overly cruel. You can test yourself by evaluating your mood after you listen to your inner critic for a few minutes. Does it improve or worsen? Does listening to the critic lead to more effective action or to paralysis and self-doubt? This assessment can help illustrate your critic's role in your mood.

In mindfulness classes that we've taught for over fifteen years, one of the first meditations we teach is the body scan. We know from experience that a sizable percentage of people will doze off during that first meditation experience. However, whether they fall asleep is less important than how they respond to the body-scan process. Depressed individuals commonly say, "I'm not good at this," either to themselves or to the group. Others may feel that they are "too depressed to do this" or "other group members can do this better" than they can. Such statements do not lead to an improved mood; the inner critic prevents them from benefiting from the meditation. A self-compassionate voice might say, "I'm just starting to learn about this. The teacher says it is common to fall asleep early on in the training," or "I'm glad I could give myself permission to relax and fall asleep — I don't do that very often."

This example is a relatively minor one, but what happens if you experience a true setback in life, such as being fired or laid off? If you are prone to depression, it's pretty obvious what your inner critic would say: "You are a failure, and you'll never find another job." We all know, though, that getting fired or laid off is usually a complex process in which many factors are operating.

A good friend of mine held an important leadership position for more than ten years. He was widely recognized and respected. Then the organization he was with had a change at the top and shifted emphasis to new areas. The executive leadership decided he was no longer the man for the job. He was let go. He had enough self-compassion to feel good about his span of leadership, and he was able to say to himself that he wasn't a failure, that the organization's focus had changed. He was still able to see that he was a competent person.

The important part of self-compassion is that you are able to continue to regard yourself with kindness despite changes in the external situation. If you can do so, your sense of yourself will be less vulnerable to messages from others telling you differently. And you'll come to see that it isn't necessarily events that determine our mood; it's the attitude we take toward them.

If you suffer from depression, it is not easy to be kind to yourself. The depression itself interferes with being compassionate toward yourself by amplifying the self-critical voice. Depression also makes you pessimistic and fills you with hopelessness and helplessness. If you feel this way, how can you change your stance toward yourself? Aren't you stuck with the way you are?

The answer is you can change. Self-compassion is in some ways like a lens. If the mindful awareness of something — whether it is your mood, your thoughts, your sensations, or something external — is like shining a spotlight on it, then self-compassion can be considered a colored lens that you place in the light's path. It softens the image and allows a different take on the issue. Mindful awareness is the first step in the process, followed by applying a self-compassionate lens. This lens helps buffer the impact of negative events.

Self-compassion and mindfulness can be seen as the two wings that equanimity flies on. Equanimity, a key goal in many meditation traditions, is the even-keeled composure that allows you to respond skillfully to situations. Adding self-compassion to your mindfulness meditations will give you an opportunity to practice it and so develop your skill at it. For example, there's almost always a chance to use it when the mind wanders. When you are doing a meditation that focuses on your breath, you will undoubtedly find your attention straying. You may fall asleep or get bored. You can strengthen your self-compassion by congratulating yourself for noticing what's happened, then realize it is part of a common human experience, and gently bring your attention back to your breath.

Similarly, in your everyday life, problems, mistakes, or failures will occur. They do for all of us. When you encounter problems, try seeing them through the lens of self-compassion by asking the inner critic to step aside for a bit.

As we've mentioned, the inner critic can be especially cruel for those who are depressed. Perhaps your own parents were not very kind to you. As a consequence, you may have incorporated your parents' voice into your inner critic. By strengthening your ability to be self-compassionate, you can diminish the power of this critical voice.

People with depression do not let go of their inner critic easily. Not only have they had it for a long time, but, as mentioned above, it is often connected to important early caregivers. They may have been harsh critics, but they were also the only caregivers you had as you grew up. This means that you may be particularly attached to the critical voices. As children we tend to believe what our parents say. If we didn't, the world would be quite scary, as if there was no one at the steering wheel. But as an adult, no longer dependent on those early caregivers, you can start to pay less attention to those voices.

Additionally, you may see the critical voice as one that will help you improve. No wonder you don't relinquish the critic so easily. Yet experience and extensive research suggest that this belief — that harsh self-criticism betters us somehow — is erroneous. And there is no empirical evidence that being self-compassionate lowers a person's standards. In research, self-compassion has been shown to have a protective function. For example, soldiers with higher self-compassion had lower rates of post-traumatic stress disorder (PTSD).[4] Other research has shown that a compassion-based therapy for those suffering PTSD leads to enhanced self-compassion and decreased self-blame.[5]

The Benefits of Self-Compassion

In depression therapy, self-compassion has also been shown to have powerful effects. Willem Kuyken and colleagues investigated the process of mindfulness-based cognitive therapy in depression. Although changes in mindfulness were important in mediating MBCT's effects, Kuyken and colleagues found that changes in self-compassion levels were at least as important in producing change. In their research, mindfulness and self-compassion both appeared to have an uplifting effect in depression.[6] Learning how to view yourself compassionately can have a powerful antidepressant effect of its own.

Learning how to view yourself compassionately can have a powerful antidepressant effect of its own.

Self-compassion has been associated with other beneficial health effects. For example, in studies of college students with higher self-compassion levels, smoking rates are lower and exercise rates are higher.[7] It appears that treating yourself more kindly also manifests in healthy behaviors. Self-compassion has also been associated with improved coping in individuals with chronic diseases such as inflammatory bowel disease and celiac disease.[8]

The beneficial effects of self-compassion are not tied to self-esteem. Self-esteem is based on an evaluation of your self-worth, but, as we've seen, evaluations are prone to distortions. With self-compassion, you don't have to think of yourself as a genius to treat yourself in a kindly way. This feature may be at the heart of self-compassion's beneficial effects. You may be wondering if you can really make a shift in your self-compassion levels. Our experience with teaching MBCT to hundreds of participants is that you can. In fact, in our research there was a noticeable increase in self-compassion after eight weeks.

In a particularly insightful paper entitled "The Place of Action in Personality Change," written years ago, psychiatrist Allen Wheelis describes how change takes place in a person.[9] Rather than a process that happens rapidly, he likened personality change to the flow of water from an alpine crater lake that has one outlet. If you want the water to flow out somewhere else, you have to put the effort into digging the outlet elsewhere. It's hard at first, but once the digging level is lower than the original outlet, the water itself will take over the work of cutting the path out. It is a useful model for understanding the process of change and how new neural pathways can be developed. It is not easy to start applying self-compassion, but as you do the "digging," it will become progressively easier. And the benefits will be obvious.

Building self-compassion is like building another skill or a muscle; it can be strengthened with practice, for example, by doing the following meditation.

TRY THIS: Building Self-Compassion

Sit with the eyes closed and focus on the breath flowing in and out through the nostrils for a minute or two.

Notice whatever thoughts are occurring without trying to change or judge them.

Then notice the feelings that may be accompanying the thoughts. Name the feelings when you become aware of them.

Put your hand on your heart, and aim the same kindness you

would show toward a small child toward yourself as you repeat each
of the following phrases with successive breaths:

> *May I be safe.*
> *May I be healthy.*
> *May I be happy.*
> *May I live with ease.*

(If you find it difficult to say these things to yourself, start by saying them to someone about whom you are completely unambivalent,
such as a loved one, an infant, or even a pet, before you move on to
yourself.)

Continue this repetition for five minutes.

9

ACHIEVEMENTS DIVIDED BY EXPECTATIONS EQUALS HAPPINESS

Depression has been considered a discrepancy-based illness. That is, you want something to be other than the way it is. At times setting high expectations can be helpful in enhancing motivation. In depression, however, we tend to set them so high that they are not achievable. Such impossible ideals lead to the self-criticism that is a hallmark of depression. Having a mindful perspective of your own achievements and expectations can be important in regulating your own mood.

You may have an expectation about yourself, such as "I should be thinner (or smarter or wealthier or more accomplished, etc.) than I am." Because of this drive to be different from the way you are, you may feel deficient, defective, and lacking. This sense of defectiveness has many consequences, such as not feeling able to succeed in a variety of ways. "How can I find a mate if I'm so defective? Even if I find one, he or she will soon find out about my deficiencies and leave me, so why even bother to try?" This habit of comparing yourself to an idealized self-concept and finding that you come up short often leads to a pervasive sense of your inadequacy as a person.

Albert was just starting to learn meditation in one of my

MBCT groups. He had just completed a walking meditation for the first time. This involved walking slowly and paying attention to the sensations in his lower limbs. The instruction was that if the mind wandered, he was to gently escort the attention back to the lower limbs. Because of the slow pace, people often feel unsteady in the beginning. At the end of the meditation, Albert reported feeling very shaky and being sure he was doing something wrong. He had been preoccupied with trying to correct his walking. His expectation was that he should be "doing it right" and that he was failing because of his unsteadiness. He held this expectation despite the advice that there was no one right way and that many people felt clumsy when they first tried the meditation. Eventually he came to see that the expectation of perfection in walking was similar to other ways in which he criticized himself.

Keys to Diminishing Depression and Increasing Happiness

One model of happiness says happiness is equal to achievements (your view of yourself, or self-concept) divided by expectations (your fantasied ideal self):

$$\text{Happiness} = \frac{\text{Achievements}}{\text{Expectations}}$$

Because people with depression tend to set their expectations so high, no matter what they actually achieve, they end up feeling poorly about themselves.

Let's examine this equation in more detail. In addition to setting the expectation bar very high, another one of the traps in depression is that people tend to minimize their achievements. This minimization of accomplishments lays the groundwork for unhappiness. The way to diminish this effect is to develop the ability to more realistically assess the achievements.

But because achievements tend to be relatively fixed within age ranges in life, what is probably more variable in this equation are expectations. For example, a physician could be an excellent clinician but feel inadequate because he had failed to win a Nobel Prize in medicine. The expectation in this case was so inflated that his real achievement was always going to fall short.

If we could make it a reasonable expectation to be "good enough," not perfect, it would be much easier to feel good about ourselves. That's a big leap for some of us. The depressive combination of diminishing our view of our achievements and inflating our expectations is so entrenched, that it keeps the number for the happiness side of the equation lower than it might otherwise be. Perfection is the enemy of the good. Striving for perfection can be paralyzing, while achieving the good can be satisfying.

Perfection is the enemy of the good. Striving for perfection can be paralyzing, while achieving the good can be satisfying.

One fellow I was treating for depression told me he wanted to be the absolute best professor at his university. He had recently returned to work after several months of depression-related disability leave. In his work there was no way to determine who the "best" was and no likelihood that such an expectation would ever realistically be met. In such a situation he was setting himself up for feeling worse about himself.

Seeking perfection can even apply to meditation. For example, if you go into meditation aiming to make sure your mind never wanders, you will inevitably be disappointed. Minds wander. This is why learning meditation is considered a *practice*. There is no perfect meditation with rock-solid focus.

This point was illustrated in a walking meditation done by a small group of six members. In walking meditation, the idea is to focus the attention on the sensations in the lower limbs; if the mind wanders, the attention is to be gently escorted back to the sensations. After the group completed the meditation, all six members believed they had not done it "right." They noticed being unsteady or having pain in their hips, knees, or feet. All of these responses are not unusual in meditative walking. Some members thought they were not maintaining the proper distance from others as they walked around the room in an oval. Some thought others were doing the meditation better than they were. One member had noticed how he had started ruminating about a problem at work.

In discussion the members understood that they had exaggerated their expectations and minimized their accomplishment. The primary focus in the meditation is to stay upright and notice what sensations are present; there was nothing to be achieved here other than just being. Yet all six members of the group had allowed their minds to drift to self-critical thoughts, and their expectations of being other than they were had led them to be disappointed. But noticing how their minds had drifted in this direction also allowed them to see that shifting their ideas of achievement and expectations could lead to change.

Impaired Self-Concept

In her book *Radical Acceptance*, meditation teacher and psychologist Tara Brach notes that in many individuals the sense of unworthiness takes on the quality of a trance. It's as if they are hypnotized into believing themselves to be unworthy.[1] To the outside observer they may appear to be fine. But in their mind they suffer as much as subjects hypnotized into believing they are a chicken. Typically, unrealistic expectations drive this sense of unworthiness.

With depression, depressive ideas often lead to such impaired self-concepts that one develops an almost delusional view of one-self. This view includes a sense of unworthiness, incompetency, and defectiveness as a person. This in turn leads to a fear of rela-tionships, failure, and the future.

In an example of how our experience of life can differ de-pending on our basic frame of mind, we can look to Jim. He was a journeyman electrician who was well regarded by his peers. When his company took on a new large project, Jim's boss asked him to become a supervisor. Jim's self-image was so faulty that he initially felt his boss was trying to set him up to fail, so he could get rid of him. Only after much discussion with his friends did he accept the fact that the promotion was actually recognition of his expertise.

Rewriting Expectations

The principles of the happiness equation first occurred to me when I was a consultant to the medical-surgical intensive-care unit (ICU) at our hospital.[2] I met with the nurses weekly to help them cope with the high stress of the ICU. In the ICU, death is a constant. Once, several patients died in a short period of time, and a number of the nurses became depressed. They felt disap-pointed about their work, and some even thought about changing careers. In our weekly support group, we examined their feel-ings about the deaths. A number of the nurses voiced the idea that they should be able to save every patient who comes through the door. This meant that even if they saved 95 percent of the patients and 5 percent died, they could not feel good. They were helping so many people and doing heroic work, but because their expectations were so high, extending to 100 percent, they did not feel very good about themselves.

After discussions, they began to shift their expectations. They could do the best they possibly could, they realized, and still lose some patients who were just too sick to save. And these patients they could help die with dignity and provide support to the family during that process. In this way, by shifting their expectations to more reasonable levels, they could start to feel good about their continuing work, even though they could not prevent every death.

It is critically important to understand that lowering or changing your expectations does not mean giving up on ever again attempting to excel or resigning yourself to mediocrity. It means starting to assess the situation and responding to it in a skillful way. You have to use judgment about when you choose to modify your expectation level. Just remember that in individuals with depression, the default selection is to choose expectations that are often perfectionist and unrealistic.

This whole concept often trips people up. They say, "If I let go of my high expectations, I might fall flat. My high expectations are what got me to where I am today." To this I say yes, this is true, and there's nothing wrong with striving, but I don't think you need to worry about dropping your high expectations overnight. We're talking about shifting your perspective and having compassion for yourself.

Take the meditation process itself. If you practice some meditation every day, you will begin to notice that the days can be quite different from one another, even if you are doing exactly the same guided meditation. One day you may say to yourself, "Wow, I was really focused today," and on another day, "I really wandered all over today." You might say, "Nothing happened today. I even fell asleep." So if you expect to be really focused every day, you could feel a sense of failure on a day when you did not feel focused.

Having the expectation, "My mind will be different every day, so I can accept whatever is present and feel good about that," changes the perception dramatically. This involves letting go of the doing mode, where you are trying to achieve something specific, and moving to the being mode, where you accept things as they are that day. One day you may feel like a novice meditator and the next day like an expert; all I am suggesting is that you change your perspective and see such variations as perfectly normal.

Let's look at another way the happiness equation can lead to the trap of depression. A woman wanted to go dancing, but felt she could not do so because she thought she was overweight. The trap of her depressive thinking was her thought that she had to be different than the way she perceived herself to be in order to start doing things she might enjoy. She found through mindfulness practice that this thought was just a thought and that she could go ahead and go dancing, even though she did not feel she was at her perceived ideal weight. The trap was her feeling a need to change before she could do something. This was the opposite of what would be most helpful for her: if she went ahead and went dancing, it might be fun and actually lead to a change in her self-concept.

One way of assessing whether you are being realistic is to look at how you are using expectations in your everyday life. I'm talking about bringing a mindful perspective to your thinking processes. If you are battering yourself with self-criticism, you probably have high and unrealistic expectations. For example, perhaps you say, "I should never make a mistake." Everybody makes mistakes. That is the hallmark of humanity. If your expectation is perfection and you are using it to be self-critical, then that is a clue that you are in the territory of unrealistic expectations. You are not setting a goal for yourself that will enhance your achievement or your happiness. Depression leads to faulty ideas that need to be countered with action before your self-concept can improve.

> Depression leads to faulty ideas that need to be countered with action before your self-concept can improve.

One of the difficulties in depression is the amplified discrepancy between your idea of yourself, how you think you are, and an idealized self, how you think you should be. Psychologist Clayton Barbeau coined the term "should yourself" to describe this. Some people say one of the most common features of depression is shoulding yourself. For example, you may think, "There is something not right with me the way I am," therefore "I should be something else." When you should yourself, you are saying, "I should be other than the way I am." One way of softening the should statement is to replace the word *should* with the phrase *it would be nice if.* For example, "It would be nice if I were thinner (richer, wiser, etc.)." It takes the edge off the absolute demand on yourself.

The automatic negative thoughts that accompany depression will often accelerate downward spirals of mood. Mindfully observing the thought process may allow an interruption of the spiral. When you start shoulding, it may help to think of Sitting Bull's comment, "Each creature is good in the sight of the great spirit. It is not necessary for an eagle to become a crow." You can then awaken to your life here and now, as it is.

Elizabeth came into the MBCT group with the expectation that she would stop having anxiety completely, that the thoughts producing her anxiety would stop entirely. Her anxious thoughts included ideas that her children were headed for catastrophe. She came to realize, however, that she would likely never completely eliminate anxiety-producing thoughts. However, she learned to tune them out.

As she practiced her meditation, she became familiar with being able to label her thoughts — for example, "There's an anxiety thought" — so that instead of reacting to them, she was able to view them from a distance. Rather than being in the forefront of her mind, they were in the background. At times they would rise more to the fore, but when they did, she could identify them as thoughts and not facts. She also began to notice that when she was feeling anxious, it did not mean anything was necessarily wrong; it was just her mind generating these thoughts and feelings.

In her process of gaining perspective, Elizabeth particularly liked one analogy first described by Steven C. Hayes in his work on acceptance and commitment therapy.[3] Suppose you are having a party. You've been planning it for months and have invited all of your friends. You haven't invited Aunt Bessie, because you don't like her very much. She's mean, critical, and insulting and never brings a thing to family gatherings. So you are enjoying your party with your friends, and who do you see coming up your sidewalk? Aunt Bessie!

What do you do? Go to the front door and struggle to hold it shut against her efforts to get in? If you do that, what happens to your ability to enjoy your party? It's gone, because you are locked in a struggle with Aunt Bessie. If you let her in, the party might suffer a wee bit, but for the most part you can still enjoy your many friends. In this analogy, Aunt Bessie is a representation of your depression or anxiety. The more you struggle to keep it out, the more you are taken away from being able to enjoy your party — in this case the ability to pursue your life's goals and values. If you are more allowing, some depression or anxiety may be present, but you can still go in the direction you want.

Elizabeth was able to shift her relationship to her thoughts and realize that her mind, although generating anxiety, did not have to be a roadblock to moving ahead in her life. She no longer felt the need to respond to these thoughts as she had before. Mindfulness gave her the capacity to identify the thoughts as they were emerging and to be able to respond skillfully rather than reactively. Moreover, by practicing letting go of thoughts and bringing the attention back to the breath, she was often able to learn that she did not have to follow the thoughts indefinitely. She became empowered with greater capacity to focus her attention where she chose to. She learned that she could not control her thoughts as they emerged into her consciousness, but she could choose how she would respond to them.

The role of expectations is illustrated by the story of the farmer and the Buddha. A farmer came to visit the Buddha for advice. He described his problems at length, starting with the fact that he loved farming, but had been troubled by drought in some years and excessive rain in others, which made it hard for him to produce his crops consistently. The Buddha replied that he could not help the farmer with this problem.

The farmer went on to tell the Buddha that he loved his wife, but that she often made comments that displeased him very much. He then talked about his children, whom he also loved, but they often disappointed him and would not do what he asked them. The Buddha said he could not help with any of the family problems the farmer described.

The farmer was very disappointed, told the Buddha he had not helped him at all, and then turned to leave. The Buddha then asked the farmer if he wanted help with the problem the Buddha had identified. The farmer asked what the problem was. The Buddha answered that the farmer expected never to have any of the problems he had initially described. The Buddha explained that if the farmer gave up such expectations, he would be much happier.

Like the farmer's wish for no problems, an infinite list of fulfilled expectations is not achievable. As long as we hang on to our long lists of expectations, we will feel disappointed.

Another analogy that can help us here has to do with ocean waves. If a large wave is coming, the best way to deal with it is not to outrace it by turning to the side and swimming rapidly; such an action is usually futile. Rather, the best thing to do is dive headlong into it and come through the wave. In some respects, this is like opening the door to Aunt Bessie.

In fact, the wave analogy is quite useful as an illustration of having a mindful perspective about thoughts and feelings. If you stand in ocean water for a while, you will find that waves will continually come at you. The first time, they may actually knock you over. You may feel the force of the waves pounding against you, and it may be troubling. With time, however, you will realize that, yes, waves come and go. They will no longer be a surprise. Their impact is something that you can expect. In this way, you become better able to stand despite the oncoming waves and may come to realize they have less ferocity than you first thought. Of course, this analogy itself is not perfect, because some waves can be lethal, and it may be prudent to get completely out of the water! Mindful awareness helps provide a skillful response to the situation.

Physical and Cognitive Symptoms

Depression has physical symptoms such as fatigue, loss of energy, altered sleep patterns, altered appetite, and a sense of being slowed down or agitated. It also has cognitive symptoms such as thoughts of guilt, worthlessness, and hopelessness. These cognitive symptoms are just as much part of the depressive package as the physical symptoms. Unfortunately, they are often not recognized as such, and people tend to believe them as if they were facts. For example, a depressed person considers the thought "The future is hopeless" a fact rather than a symptom. Understanding that the mind is often not a friend helps us to realize that this is a thought and not a fact.

Michelle said that in the past she had thought of depression as happening to her, instead of seeing it as related to the way she was thinking. When she became aware that it was her thoughts about events, not the events themselves, that were determining her mood, her experience shifted. Her mindful awareness of her thoughts helped lead her to change her perspective.

The single most important change for Michelle was in the locus of control. She moved from thinking that her experience arose from something outside of herself to realizing it was internal. This allowed her to feel some sense of control; it was empowering. She no longer saw herself as just being buffeted by interactions or events.

This shift from feeling you have no control — over events or your mood — to feeling that you have some control has a powerful antidepressant effect of its own. The effects of this shift in the perceived locus of control have been demonstrated clinically in individuals treated in psychotherapy.

Juliet described one particular incident as helping her understand her thoughts and their relationship to her mood. She had come home one afternoon and found that she did not have her key. She also did not have her cell phone with her, so she could not call her husband. She became upset, which was made all the worse by the thought that her husband was out sailing with friends and unreachable. She found herself getting increasingly angry at him for not being available to rescue her. Thinking that he wouldn't be home for five more hours, she had plenty of time to focus on her anger. Soon anger turned into feeling depressed, with the thought that she had purposely been betrayed. Here she was, abandoned by her husband, who was out enjoying himself while she suffered.

She had been standing outside the apartment for close to an hour, getting more and more angry and depressed, when her husband suddenly opened the door from the inside. He'd been there the entire time. When he opened the door and saw her, he told her how worried he had been when she hadn't come home. As she processed what had happened and realized how angry and depressed she had gotten about feeling rejected and abandoned, she also recognized that this was a familiar story line for her. Instead of being self-compassionate and forgiving herself for making a human error such as forgetting her key, she would often construct a scenario of being wronged as a way of shifting responsibility to someone else and playing out her familiar story.

Self-compassion often leads to greater acceptance of oneself. Applying the lens of self-compassion softens our view of ourselves even when we detect a discrepancy in what we hoped for. This meditation offers one approach to bringing a gentleness to our view of ourselves.

TRY THIS: Self-Compassion and Acceptance Meditation

While seated or standing, close your eyes and focus on the breath moving in and out of your nostrils.

Notice the sensations present in the body, such as contact points with the chair or your feet with the floor.

Then bring to mind a behavior in your life that you would like to change. Don't select a major life-changing behavior when you first try this meditation; choose a small habit or tendency you'd like to change.

Notice what you say to yourself about this behavior. What does your inner critic say? How do you feel? The inner critic may want you to change, perhaps by being perfect, but does criticizing yourself help?

Apply self-compassion to the behavior. Start by thanking the inner critic for suggesting that you change. Ask the inner critic to step aside and make room for your more compassionate self.

Bring in your more compassionate self. This self sees the problematic behavior but wants to change not because you are a bad person, but because change would lessen your suffering. Ask your more compassionate self, "What advice would I give to a friend with this problem?" or "What would my most compassionate friend or mentor say to me about the problem?"

After you have answered these questions, return your focus to your breathing for a few minutes and then come back to the present moment in the room.

THE DIFFERENCE BETWEEN PAIN AND SUFFERING

According to Buddhist teacher Shinzen Young, pain, whether it is physical or emotional, is inevitable in life. It is our resistance to accepting pain that produces much of the suffering we experience.[1] A shorthand way of describing this is the equation:

Suffering = Resistance × Pain

The more we resist the pain, the greater the suffering. You may be thinking, "Isn't it natural to resist an unpleasant situation? If I don't resist depression, won't I be overwhelmed by it?" With depression, the word *resistance* refers to the tendency to avoid anything that might activate or worsen depressed feelings. In some ways this is like trying to cover a bruise, so it won't be touched and have the pain worsened. The bandage may help prevent more bruising, but at the cost of restriction of function.

With depression, you might avoid relationships out of a fear that they will end in rejection. You might avoid demanding jobs for fear that they might expose imagined incompetencies. You might actively avoid success for fear of the embarrassment of a future failure. You might avoid difficult people by staying at home. You might numb the pain of depression with drugs or alcohol.

These avoidance strategies, contrary to their intention, are more likely to keep you stuck in depression or even amplify it than offer any sustained relief. Moreover, when you use these strategies, they build progressively toward a more restricted, lonelier life. Avoiding relationships and responsible jobs leads to progressive restrictions. Once you start to avoid potential exposures to experiencing depression, even the exposures you initially accepted may become threatening. The tender bruise you are trying to protect doesn't go away; it rules your life.

Avoidance strategies are more likely to keep you stuck in depression or even amplify it than offer any sustained relief.

Jean's experience highlights this problem. Jean was chronically depressed for a number of years. She would attempt to develop new romantic relationships, but whenever she did, she went into them expecting to be rejected. She would enter these relationships desperate to be accepted, yet the pattern of rejections continued. Whenever a new romantic interest made a remark or gesture that she interpreted as critical, she believed that the rejection had begun again.

Her mind told her she needed to fix the problem and avoid rejection by being more submissive. But her efforts to do so invariably backfired, and she became angry that her sacrifices hadn't worked. Her anger ultimately faded as she spiraled deeper into depression, and she stopped even attempting new relationships.

As she learned mindfulness meditation, she became willing to risk experiencing the pain of rejection. She became aware of how her mind was generating stories about what would happen in her relationships. Once she realized that her stories were just thoughts and not facts, she became more willing to try dating again. She did not have to remain isolated out of avoidance. Awareness and the willingness to expose herself to risks brought her freedom to pursue relationships again.

Anxiety functions in much the same way. Take panic disorder as an example. As we saw with Kathy in Chapter 6, a panic attack does not automatically produce panic disorder. It only becomes a disorder when the fear of another panic attack becomes an overarching organizing factor in a person's life. In this situation, the person begins to avoid situations where panic episodes occurred in an attempt to avoid another attack. Settings such as stores, malls, or other public places where easy escape is not possible if another attack occurs often become off limits. As time goes on, the spread of avoidance increases, and the person may become unable to leave the house. Studies indicate that these avoidance behaviors, not the panic attacks themselves, are what induce most of the disability in both physical and emotional pain states.

The Additional Layer of Emotional Suffering

Robert Sapolsky, mentioned earlier in connection with the effect of mindfulness practice on the alarm areas of the brain, has also looked at suffering in both animals and humans and notes that in humans there is an additional layer of suffering beyond the physical. He calls such suffering in humans *adventitious*, meaning "added on to."[2] For example, if a bear gets a thorn in its paw, it does not generate questions such as "Why me?" or "What did I do to deserve this?" The bear experiences the painful physical sensation, but does not have the added layer of suffering that humans do as thinking and ruminating take over. Human brain studies have indicated that the pain sensations are located in one area of the brain, but that additional areas are associated with this overlay component as well.

For humans, accepting emotional pain without amplifying it is just as difficult as doing so with physical pain. For example, individuals start to recover from panic disorder not when they stop having the panic attacks, but when they can begin to accept them as just panic attacks and not a horrible catastrophe. When they can begin to label an episode as a panic attack and not a heart attack or their mind going crazy, their suffering begins to diminish.

The same holds true for depression. There is unequivocal emotional pain in depression, and resistance to the pain often amplifies the suffering. This resistance can take many forms. People may try to avoid pain in the form of denial, attempt to suppress it with substance use, or manifest compulsive behaviors as attempts to cope. The attitudes about depression, similar to the fear of panic attacks, can add to the suffering. "Depression means I am a weak person." "Depression means I am a moral failure." "This means I will be this way forever." "I will always let my family down with my illness." Self-critical statements like these worsen the suffering. What is important to realize here is that it's not just the initial emotional pain but the overlay we place on it that produces much of our suffering.

In another illustration of how we amplify our suffering, pain researcher Henry Beecher and colleagues studied soldiers wounded while landing on the beaches of Anzio, Italy, in World War II.[3] They compared the wounded soldiers' experiences with male civilians receiving gall-bladder surgery back in the United States. Beecher matched the soldiers and civilians by age, past illness, and the amount of tissue destruction. The soldiers had extensive wounds, but only a minority of them said they had enough pain to warrant medications. Overall, 32 percent of the military group, compared to 83 percent of the civilian group, requested narcotics. Beecher noted that there was no dependable relationship between the extent of tissue injury and the pain experienced. The *meaning* of the wound appeared to be the primary factor differentiating the two samples. The soldiers experienced relief from the theater of war, while the civilians experienced interruption of their everyday life.

How Fear Factors In

Fear is an important overlay with pain. Research on physical pain indicates that fear of experiencing the pain is the primary determinant of how much disability the individual has. Fear drives individuals to seek substances like opioids and sometimes pursue needless surgery. With fear of emotions, the effects may also be profound. Fear of an object produces phobias, fear of other people produces social anxiety, fear of panic attacks produces panic disorder, and fear of reexperiencing traumatic events produces post-traumatic stress disorder. Fear of depression leads to a constricted life.

The relationship between suffering, resistance, and pain can be seen in everyday situations. Imagine you begin having pain in one tooth on a Friday afternoon. You call your dentist late in the afternoon and find out that he or she is out of town until Monday. What happens to your pain? Most likely it continues to bother you and may even increase in intensity over the weekend. But what happens if the situation is somewhat different?

Imagine that you call your dentist late Friday afternoon, and he or she says to come in first thing on Saturday morning. You experience relief. Often by the time you come in the next morning, the pain is either gone or so muted that you cannot even identify which tooth it was that was hurting you. Once you heard that you could see the dentist first thing in the morning, resistance to the pain immediately decreased, you accepted it, and your suffering diminished. Presumably the tooth problem causing the original pain did not disappear, but your attitude about the sensations changed dramatically.

One MBCT group member shared her problem with back pain. Donna saw her back pain as a sign of old age and decrepitude rather than as a treatable or temporary condition. She explained that she felt depressed about her physical decline. The suffering was not just due to the pain; how she interpreted the pain was causing much of it. This is true for both physical and emotional pain. It is not just the painful stimulus that causes the suffering; more is brought on by our resistance to it. Our thoughts about it, the injustice of it, the prognosis, and what the future is expected to be like lead to much of the suffering.

It is of note that individuals who are suffering from pain, when asked to project what they expect the pain levels to be at a future time, almost uniformly expect them to be dramatically higher than they actually turn out to be at the later time. Pain studies indicate that this is a common misperception. Pain tends to level off with time and not continue to accelerate. If you can accept this, it begins to alter your resistance to pain and diminish your consequent suffering.

Functional magnetic resonance imaging has shown significant findings in individuals with chronic pain. After mindfulness training the individuals continue to have activation changes in the sensory areas of the cortex of the brain related to the body part involved with pain. However, the associated areas that were affected previous to the mindfulness training returned to normal.[4] This suggests that mindfulness, which fosters increased acceptance, decreased resistance, and awareness of the painful sensations, leads to less suffering. Psychological studies of pain states indicate fear and avoidance behaviors are the major determinants of both disability and chronicity.[5] Reducing those components can lead to improved functioning, even if the painful stimuli do not change at all.

Another way of distancing yourself from critical thoughts that emerge in your mind is to use meditation to examine their source. If you can identify a critical thought as originating from a person in your past or a person unconnected to the context in which the critical thought is now coming up, perhaps that identification alone can provide you with the distance needed to defuse that thought.

As I mentioned, once when I was meditating and focusing on my breath, my thoughts about an irritating work situation kept coming up. The critical voice told me I should have handled the situation better. I realized the critical voice behind these thoughts belonged to a colleague of mine; it was just as if she were speaking to me. Since she is not someone I usually turn to for advice, I thought, "Why should I be listening to her comments and taking them to heart?" It was almost like being cut off on the highway by a thoughtless driver — and was I going to continue to be upset about that? Consequently, the barrage of critical thoughts dropped away, and I was able to let go of the distressing emotional state I had been in.

Here is a meditation to help you identify the source of some of your critical thoughts.

TRY THIS: Labeling the Source of Critical Thoughts

Start by focusing on the breath moving in and out of the nostrils.

As you pay attention to the breath, for the next five to ten minutes notice any critical thoughts that arise, thoughts that are telling you you made a mistake, should have done something better, or otherwise didn't measure up.

Isolate one comment that disturbs you the most. Who does that sound like? Who has said that to you in the past? Is there any reason to heed that person today? Who has said that to you in a different context? Is there any reason to think it applies to this context?

Whether originally well-meaning or not, those words are no longer helpful. No matter who is saying them, relegate them elsewhere. You have moved beyond them. Make the choice to no longer let them have power in your life.

ACCEPTANCE AND OTHER SHIFTS IN ATTITUDE

11

We are just as likely to try to avoid painful mental states as physical ones. These attempts paradoxically often amplify the pain. Think of a situation in which you have to do a task that you are not fond of. An example in the medical setting might be when resident doctors (doctors in training) have to be on call in the hospital. Many residents find aspects of being on call unpleasant, such as not getting as much sleep as usual and having to deal with urgent situations. For those residents who strenuously dislike and try to avoid being on call as much as possible, the suffering associated with it is substantial. Other residents, however, put up little resistance. They see being on call as an opportunity to have a learning experience and autonomy. These residents experience little suffering and handle the task of being on call in a positive manner.

The acceptance of emotional pain caused by depression is not the same as resignation. Resignation occurs when the individual says there is nothing to be done about a situation that is occurring: "I can't change it, so I just have to suffer." Acceptance is different. It admits the existence of something, but doesn't foreclose what happens after that acknowledgment; the end result is open.

Accepting the situation is actually the first step in being able to change it.

For example, as long as those with an alcohol-abuse problem deny they have a problem, they will be unable to make any progress toward treating it. If they do manage to admit to the problem but then shut the door, so to speak, on the end result, they have fallen into resignation: "I am an alcoholic, and there's nothing I can do about it." In contrast, open-ended acceptance is the first step toward treatment of the problem. Individuals can then engage in a number of different possible treatment approaches. They can go to Alcoholics Anonymous, stop drinking, or enter an inpatient or outpatient treatment program. Acceptance allows them to respond skillfully to the situation and take steps to change it if they desire to.

Acceptance is counterintuitive when it comes to unpleasant experiences like depression and anxiety. Who wants them? Usually we try to get as far away as possible from them. However, this does not actually work too well with these unpleasant states of mind. They tend to be "sticky" and difficult to escape from.

Remember trying to pull your fingers out of a Chinese finger trap? The harder you pull, the more stuck your fingers become. The key to escaping is to gently move the fingers together and then ease them out. The same factors apply with states of mind. Neuroscience researcher Richard Davidson, at the University of Wisconsin, has found that avoidance techniques activate the right dorsolateral prefrontal cortex, one of the main areas associated with increased depression and anxiety.[1] Acceptance approaches, on the other hand, activate the left dorsolateral prefrontal cortex. That area is associated with relief of depression and is the area activated in a new depression treatment, transcranial magnetic stimulation. Mindfulness meditation also leads to increased activation of the left dorsolateral prefrontal cortex. It has brain effects consistent with neuroscience findings associated with relieving depression and anxiety.

Acceptance means allowing things to be as they are. Sometimes you may find it hard to accept a situation. In these instances, it may help to use the words *acknowledgment of* or *willingness to experience* a situation. Acceptance actually puts you in a position to make a skillful response to whatever is present.

We can see that usually it is not the biological pain itself that causes most of the suffering we experience. Rather, it is our resistance to it — attempts to avoid it, suppress it, or distract ourselves from it. In accepting pain, our resistance decreases, and the consequent suffering does as well. Odd as it may sound, you might try welcoming the depression or anxiety: "There you are, my old acquaintance." When you do this, it is like opening the door of your "guest house." Also, as one participant of MBCT said, keeping the door closed is an illusion, because there really is no door.

A Mindful Approach to Pain

One technique for dealing with pain involves trying to remove as much of the cause of the pain as possible. For example, the bear in the woods with a thorn in its paw might pull the thorn out. If it couldn't do so, the bear would be stuck with the pain, but it wouldn't do "human" things like blaming itself or someone else. If you can pull your thorn out, do so. For depression, this might mean getting out of a troublesome work or personal relationship that has you feeling trapped. If you can't get out of the situation, then apply mindfulness to the pain. You can be mindful of the pain the same way you are mindful of the breath.

Note the quality of the pain, the intensity, and how the pain changes moment to moment. Note the thoughts that arise in association with the pain. Try shining the spotlight of mindfulness on the pain and see if it brings acceptance. Mindfulness also brings present-moment awareness. Much of the suffering of pain is due to negative thoughts such as "This will continue to increase," "This means I'm a weak person," or "I can't stand this anymore." These thoughts occur even while you are tolerating the pain in the moment and even when it is at a stable level of intensity. Having pain certainly does not mean you are weak.

I have already mentioned my success with meditation for migraines. The first time, I initially fell under the sway of the pain. I told myself I couldn't stand it. I projected that I would not be able to give an important talk the next day, because pain would disable me. Then I began to apply mindfulness to the situation. I realized that I *was* standing the pain. When I focused on just the present moment, I noticed that I *was* tolerating it. I noticed that I was projecting a negative outcome in the future and that I could let that thought go and return to the present. Finally, I could decenter by observing myself having pain: "There's Stu having pain." With that perspective, my suffering decreased dramatically. The pain was still present, but it was as though I was looking through a window on it instead of being fused with it.

In reality, pain tends to level off at a certain point and stop increasing. That is not to say that it's pleasant, but the fears of unceasing and increasing pain are not warranted. And accepting the pain may actually diminish all the projections about it. Accepting it, just as it is, gives you a different perspective about what you can do about it. If you can focus on the pain sensations in the present moment, the weight of the suffering may be significantly lessened.

This applies to the pain of depression. One of the most distressing aspects about depression is getting depressed about being depressed and fearing getting more depressed. If you suffer from depression, you will typically have a lot of thoughts about it: "This is going to get worse." "This will go on forever." When these thoughts occur and you do not realize they are thoughts and not facts, it is easy to see how they could lead to more depression.

One woman taking a mindfulness course said, "I had a swarm of negative thoughts as I tried to meditate." Initially she accepted the thoughts as if they were true. Had she been resigned to the truth of those thoughts, her depression might have increased: "Now I know a lot about my shortcomings and that is even more depressing." With mindfulness, however, she began to realize that her mind was really generating that swarm of negative ideas. She started to change her relationship to these thoughts and stopped trying to cease having the thoughts. She began to see that her thoughts about depression and its apparent invincibility didn't have to come true and were not cast-iron facts.

This shift in attitude toward thoughts demonstrates one of the important elements of the mindfulness approach. In traditional cognitive therapy, you might catch yourself having a depressive thought and try to discern what type of distortion was taking place in that thought. Then you would develop an alternate or more balanced thought to replace the negative one. With the mindfulness approach, there is no replacement of one thought with another. You simply recognize that it is just a thought and then are able to let it go without attaching validity to it. If you can let go of a wandering thought while you are focusing on the breath, you can let go of a depressive thought as well.

Assessing the Accuracy of Your Thoughts

One mindfulness participant asked a question about how you differentiate accurate thoughts from false ones. She said, "If I look at myself in the mirror, I see myself as fat. I think that's an accurate thought." One way of assessing your thoughts is to use objective measures; in this case the woman could weigh herself. But objective measures often fall short, because depressed individuals have an arsenal of rationalizations to prove the authenticity of the negative thoughts. For example, "Even though my weight is normal, I am really obese because I have very small bones."

One of the most useful techniques we have found to help individuals trying to discern fact from falsehood is asking them to take a look at how the thoughts are being used. If the thought is one that you are berating yourself with and you feel worse after thinking it, there is a good likelihood that it is related to your depression. You can sharpen this assessment by asking yourself how you feel when having the thought. For example, when you have the thought "I am fat," how do you feel? If you feel bad or more depressed, this is good presumptive evidence that the thought is coming from your depressive mind, the mind that is not your friend.

Your mind can be particularly good at generating fear-inducing thoughts. These can be related to a real, dangerous situation, but if you suffer from depression or anxiety, there is a good chance that your fearful thoughts are coming from that mind that is not your friend. An acronym that helps unpack the concept of fear is False Evidence Appearing Real. Such FEAR often drives individuals to avoid situations that would otherwise be helpful in ameliorating depression. For example, if you are depressed and stay home from a party because you don't think anybody will want to talk to you there, this behavior forecloses the possibility that you might have a positive social interaction.

What can you do when faced with fearful thoughts? Earlier we suggested that the most skillful response to a toothless lion's loud roar might be to run toward it. The same is true of emotional pain. People with panic disorder will often do best to return to the places and situations where they have had panic attacks and realize that what they are experiencing is only a panic attack and not a disaster. The same holds true for depression. Instead of avoiding interactions with others because of the fear of rejection, approaching others is one avenue for recovery. Avoiding people cuts you off from social relationships that might improve your depression. Typically, once you can view negative thoughts with a mindful perspective, you'll see that you don't have to allow them to drive your behavior.

The Mind as Weather

Many of our MBCT participants report a new ability to see their mind as similar to the weather. They come to see the mental state as temporary, not the permanent prison they formerly assumed it to be while mired in depression. For example, learning to say, "It's depressing out today" shifts the whole feeling tone of the moment. No longer are *you* depressed. You are simply having depressing thoughts or feelings today. It's depressing out today, but that doesn't mean every day will be like that.

Jennifer described a shift in attitude about depression. She explained that she had tapered off all antidepressants, because she was considering getting pregnant but was uncertain how she would cope being off medication completely. In the week between sessions she had felt depressed for one or two days, but instead of feeling hopeless that she was sinking into a new depressive episode, she told herself her mind was not her friend and "It was depressing out." She told herself that she had been depressed before and that this usually cleared in a few days. She reminded herself that just because she had a day or two of depression did not mean she would have to continue being depressed. In this way, she was able to avoid getting depressed about feeling depressed. By increasing her acceptance of depression as a temporary state, she suffered less. She avoided a downward spiral into further depression.

Another group member similarly described her earlier behavior: whenever she became depressed, she would sink into despair, telling herself she would probably be in that state forever. She envisioned herself being stuck all alone for the rest of her life. After discussion, she understood that such a thought would amplify any depressive feelings that were already present. She began to see that such depressive experiences were transient mental events being produced by her mind, which was not her friend. She could do the floating-leaf meditation and create an image of those thoughts like leaves floating down the river and practice watching them drift away.

Rumination Revisited

According to Julia, her depression was related to her inflammatory bowel disease. She had experienced little illness in life and had had a healthy lifestyle prior to the new problem. Despite having a treatable condition, she ruminated with questions such as "Why me?" and wondered whether she had done something wrong to bring on the illness.

As she practiced her meditation, she began to view her thoughts as the product of an unfriendly mind. As she did so, she began to ask herself, "Why not me?" She recognized that millions of people the world over suffered with similar illnesses. With this shift in mental posture, she began to feel a lift in her spirits. She realized that she had been interpreting the illness as some form of punishment rather than a medical problem needing treatment. It had not been aimed at her.

Julia noted that she had been ruminating and trying to find a solution to the problem of why she had gotten ill. She thought that she must have done something to cause her illness and the only way to solve it was to figure out what that was. Ruminating about yourself being at fault is common in depression even when in reality the problem often has very little to do with your action or inaction. There was no evidence that Julia's behavior had anything to do with the onset of her illness.

You'll recall our earlier discussion of rumination. Rumination is an important driver of depression. People often think that if they put more thought into something, they'll be able to figure it out. But rumination does not solve a problem. Rumination is trying to solve an unsolvable problem like Julia's attempt to figure out her illness. It usually involves regrets and churning over past events.

Ruminations are often centered on thoughts such as "If only I had done this differently," "If only I had asserted myself," or "If only I had made a different decision." These thoughts are based on the fantasy that you could actually go back in time and make a change to correct something that did not turn out well. These kinds of thoughts are often drivers of depressive states primarily because you cannot go back in time.

As Julia became more mindful, she began to become more aware of when she was ruminating. She then reported: "Now I have a choice, because I can choose to continue to ruminate or I can turn my attention to something else. I would do a breathing meditation and then decide whether I wanted to continue ruminating or focus on my breath. So for me, if I acknowledge it and say I am ruminating, it gives me some personal power and choice about whether I will continue that process or not."

Charles ruminated almost constantly about the idea that if he acquired enough wealth, he could "show" the teen schoolmates who ostracized him for some social missteps that they had been wrong. But his ruminations had been focused on solving an insoluble problem — changing the past. After learning the mindfulness approach and focusing on the present moment, he was gradually able to let go of the perceptions he had formed as a teen, relinquish his quest to change the past, and learn to enjoy the relationships he did have in the present.

Another woman developed a different approach. She said that when she ruminated and noticed it, she would just surrender. "It's the fight and struggle with it that really gives it more power. If I say to the thoughts, 'Okay, you are here. What do you want and what's your purpose?' I can then say, 'Okay. Thanks for coming.' It's just an internal conversation that I have, and sometimes I'm successful with it and sometimes I'm not. I feel as though the more I resist, the more it fuels the argument for me."

Acceptance means being aware of whatever is present and then allowing those thoughts, feelings, or sensations to be just as they are. In mindfulness, this awareness is accompanied by the absence of judgment or criticism. Acceptance can be considered a conscious willingness to stay in direct contact with experience. Acceptance turns toward what is and embraces it. Acceptance also includes letting go of any hope of a different past.

> *Acceptance means being aware of whatever is present and then allowing those thoughts, feelings, or sensations to be just as they are.*

Michael Singer, in his book *The Untethered Soul*, describes the way accepting some temporary discomfort can lead to change.[2] He illustrates this by describing how an invisible fence works in training dogs. In place of a physical fence, small transmitters are placed in the ground along the "fence line." These activate a small shock in the dog's collar if it starts to get too close. To avoid the discomfort of the shock, the dog learns not to get too close to the fence line and thus has the limits of its territory defined. If, on the other hand, the dog is willing to experience some discomfort and push up against the fence line, it might realize that it can break through the invisible fence and be completely free. So being willing to reduce avoidance leads to greater freedom (although this may not be so good for the owner!).

This model may also be used to describe people whose fear of increasing anxiety or depression may provide constraints in their lives. David was a young man entering a career in real-estate development. As part of his work he had to analyze business plans and prepare presentations on them. His problem was that he would become very anxious whenever he had to make a presentation to a large group. This was very troubling, because the presentations were an important part of his job. He thought of taking a less stressful job, even though his life's dream was to be in the real-estate business.

He started an MBCT class in hopes of diminishing his anxiety. The class was very helpful to him. He learned he could become more comfortable in a group setting without a disaster happening. Even more, he began to develop awareness that his thoughts about a catastrophe happening if he spoke before a group were just thoughts and not facts. Second, he accepted the notion that he didn't have to be free of anxiety to give his lectures. If David's most important life goal was to be successful in real estate, accepting that he would be faced with fears as he met his career tasks would propel him forward. As he performed his public-speaking tasks and accepted his discomfort, it progressively diminished. He gradually began to see speaking opportunities as chances to improve his potential in his real-estate career.

Not all scenarios can be reframed in the mind and then easily accepted for what they are. For example, why is it so difficult to be accepting with depression? This question may sound absurd. Who wants to accept depression? Doesn't everyone want to get rid of it? Unfortunately, most of us who have experienced depression will not be able to rid ourselves permanently and completely of depressive symptoms.

Remember that the STAR*D study described in Chapter 1 demonstrated that only 43 percent of participants were free of depression after four twelve-week antidepressant trials. This statistic highlights the importance of changing our relationship to depression. If we can accept it, we will be able to move forward with the goals and values we have for ourselves despite continuing to experience some symptoms. In fact, it is important to recognize that we don't have to be totally free of depressive symptoms in order to move forward. If we utilize an all-or-nothing model of thinking, where we are only functional when we are totally free of symptoms, we will prevent ourselves from moving on with our lives.

Fear of Acceptance

Fear plays a big part in how we perceive accepting depression. It is counterintuitive to think about accepting depression when you are actively suffering from it. Paradoxically this attitude may actually amplify your depression. Psychological studies that examined avoidance of unpleasant states demonstrate that attempts at avoidance actually strengthen the state itself.

Do you know the experiment "Don't think of an elephant"? Try it. Tell yourself, "Okay, I'm not going to think of an elephant." What are you thinking about right now? An elephant, most likely. Typically, our elephant thoughts increase dramatically when we try to exclude them. Similarly, research studies demonstrate that trying to avoid depressive thoughts and feelings may serve to amplify the states.

My point here is that instead of trying to avoid depression, you can actually turn toward it. What are the thoughts associated with it? What are the feelings? What are the bodily sensations? From the position of the observing self, can you see yourself experiencing depression? If so, it provides a decentered view of your

experience — "Ah, there's [fill in your name] experiencing depression." This gap between the experience and your decentered
view allows you to respond skillfully to the experience and not
just reflexively. For example, once you see your negative thoughts
are part of your depression and not accurate representations of
reality, it is liberating, even if only for a brief moment.

When you fail to accept things as they are, your decisions can
become very limiting and the consequences costly. Acceptance
allows us to open up our options and embrace our full potential.
Decisions that are limiting and other costs of avoidance result
from the failure to accept.

What Choices Did Depression Help You Make?

Let's identify the choices you've made that were based on depression, for example, situations or relationships that you avoided due
to depression. Depression can cast a negative tinge on many issues, from career decisions to social situations. You might have
avoided a prominent career possibility due to fear of failure and
humiliation and become even more depressed. This is one example of how avoiding potential depression can limit your life. Or
perhaps you avoided relationships because you feared you would
be hurt and rejected and become further depressed. You might
have limited yourself to an undesirable relationship, because you
thought you couldn't do any better due to your depression.

Think about your relationship with depression and how you
may have altered your life in order to prevent an exacerbation of
depression. Mindfulness can help you disengage from a struggle
to avoid depression, so you can change your relationship to it.
Instead of struggling to avoid it, you can bring mindful awareness
to what the experience is actually like.

When you are feeling depressed, for instance, what do you
notice in your body? Tightness in the shoulders or neck? Pressure

Mindfulness can help you disengage from a struggle to avoid depression, so you can change your relationship to it.

in the head? A slouch in posture? When you notice these things, see if you can actually breathe into the affected area of the body, allowing the breath to move freely in and out. You can repeat the phrase "It's okay" with each in-breath. This counters the catastrophizing that is such a common element of depression. This is just one way that mindfulness can improve how you cope with depression — noticing what it brings to you rather than trying to escape it.

Another way to bring awareness to depression is to evaluate what happens to your sense of time when you're feeling depressed. If you can let go of that dread of future depression and bring your attention to the present moment and your breath, you will likely notice a difference in your ability to accept your depression right now. You don't have to catastrophize about what's going to happen in the future, because you're just focused on the present moment and accepting it just as it is.

This is the essence of applying mindfulness to your depressive state. Recall the alien analogy. If you are here for one day before moving to another planet, it allows you to look at what is happening today without worrying about tomorrow.

As I mentioned earlier, one key aspect of mindfulness is letting go of judgment and criticism. This becomes especially important in accepting depression, since these two factors are extremely common for those in depressive states. Criticizing yourself because you are feeling depressed adds to your suffering. This is a favorite trick of the mind in depression: automatic negative thoughts such as "I'm a weak person" or "I'll always be a failure" generally deepen the depressive state. It is important to recognize that these types of thoughts are part of the common human experience and very typical of depressive states.

Take a moment to think about that. Even though you may believe that these thoughts are particular to you, they actually have been found to be universal in individuals suffering from depression. This means on any given day over one hundred million people in the world are having such thoughts. You are not alone.

Accepting things that are not under our control can be eye-opening, especially as it relates to depression. A perfect example can be found in the weather. Let's say you were planning to go on a picnic today with a friend. But when you woke up this morning, you found that it was raining, and the forecast said it would continue all day. You could get quite upset about this and say, "This is terrible" or "This is a big disappointment." In this instance you would be having difficulty accepting what is — namely, the rain.

However, using our previous weather analogy for depression, what would happen if you accepted the rain? Doing so would lead to an entirely different attitude. Sure, the rain would still interfere with your picnic, but you would be able to respond more skillfully to the situation. Perhaps you'd choose to picnic under a covered gazebo. Or you could decide to go to a movie or a museum and have an enjoyable time indoors. The ability to accept the situation allows you to be more adaptive despite the rain.

You can choose to view your depression in a similar light. You wake up in the morning feeling depressed. But instead of believing it's a disaster, you could choose to say, "It's depressing out today." In describing depression as an atmosphere you are currently inhabiting (and we all know the weather changes!) rather than a "thing" that you "have," you shift your attitude about it. This allows you to see it as a temporary process rather than an inexorable monolith that will be present forever. Of course, it does not erase the pain and unpleasant aspects of the depressive state, but it does help prevent much of the moralizing and catastrophizing that often accompany the state and lead to increased suffering.

Some say mindfulness provides a gap between the spark and the flame. In that gap you have a chance to respond to the situation skillfully rather than being caught in a knee-jerk reaction. Sometimes it may be useful to recognize that you have the ability to respond to a situation mindfully even when you are not completely free of depression. You might say, "I'd go to the party, but I am depressed and don't know if I can make it." A mindful approach might rephrase that by replacing *but* with *even though*: "I'll go to the party even though I am depressed and don't know if I can make it." By letting go of the idea that you must be totally free of depression and instead accepting your depression by saying, "This is how things are right now," you can reengage with your life.

One man who was learning mindfulness skills described an important realization: "While I was working I had an epiphany about the critical voices that I was hearing throughout the day. For me the critical voices were composed of anxious, sad, and depressed voices. They were just as beat up as I am; they were just rag dolls that were worn out. I was able to comfort myself in knowing that these voices were just as beaten down as I was. I said to myself, 'Give them some solace, peace. Each just wants to come in and hang out for a while. They probably just want some company, because they are knocking on the door so hard to get in.' That was my epiphany."

In concluding this discussion of acceptance, I want to mention a useful analogy described by psychologist Steven C. Hayes and colleagues. They offer the scenario of a bus driver trying to follow a certain route to a destination. He's disturbed, however, by a group of unruly passengers who heckle and shout at him in an attempt to force him to deviate from his preferred route. Although unpleasant, the passengers don't physically harm the driver. If the driver listens to them and deviates from his route, the passengers temporarily quiet down. But if the driver listens to them, he also doesn't get where he wants to go. At some point, if the driver wants to get to his destination, he has to decide to follow his own route, even if he has to put up with distractions from the passengers.

We could think of the bus in this analogy as the observing self, which can view the struggle between the mind (the driver) and distracting voices (the unruly passengers). When the driver accepts the unpleasant characters, but does not submit to what they say, he is able to get the bus to its destination.

Joanne described how the process of labeling her own unruly passengers was quite helpful without having to take any other action. Her most unruly passengers were anxiety and depression. Labeling them allowed her to view them more objectively, as separate from herself. This labeling can have powerful brain effects of its own. For example, J. David Creswell and colleagues studied individuals looking at emotionally evocative faces. Labeling them as compared to just observing them tended to decrease the activity of "alarm" regions in the brain such as the amygdala.[3] It appeared that applying reason and making a judgment to complete the label helped diminish the emotional stimulation of the pictures.

It is important to recognize that acceptance is not the same as approval. Acceptance means acknowledging an issue, while approval means condoning it.

Let's say you have a spouse who drinks excessively but refuses to acknowledge the problem or make any effort to change. If you

Acceptance means acknowledging an issue, while approval means condoning it.

were to approve of the behavior, you would be agreeing that it could continue unchanged in the future. Acceptance would mean acknowledging the problem and then deciding what you are going to do about it — for example, stay in the relationship, leave it, or start attending Al-Anon, the organization that helps family members cope with a relative who is an alcoholic. Acceptance means acknowledging things as they are; it gives you the freedom to act.

Here is a brief and useful breathing meditation that promotes self-acceptance. The object is to use the counting as a guide. The goal is not to count higher and higher, but rather to keep the attention focused on the breath.

TRY THIS: Counting Your Breaths

Focus on the breath moving in and out of the nostrils.

After a few minutes, begin counting each inhalation. Start at zero and go up to ten. If you reach ten, go back down to zero and start again.

If you notice your mind wandering, let go of the distraction, and begin at zero again.

Maintain the steady counting (and letting go of distractions) for a period you are comfortable with, perhaps five to ten minutes.

Notice your thoughts and feeling in response to this meditation. They may be just as important as your ability to keep your focus. You may be critical of yourself if you don't reach ten before your mind starts to wander, but most people starting out in our MBCT program only reach three! Your acceptance of your mind's tendency to wander can move you from self-criticism to self-compassion. You might tell yourself that keeping a focus is not as easy as it may seem, but you don't have to beat yourself up about it.

HOW TO LIVE WELL
DESPITE DEPRESSION

Keeping Your Practice Alive

Applying mindfulness to depression is somewhat counter to our normal tendency to avoid unpleasant situations and states of mind. Typically, with those states, we want to run away as fast as possible or push them away as strongly as possible. Bringing mindfulness to the depressive state, by contrast, calls on us to sit still and pay attention to the depressive mood.

What is present in the depressive state? A tightness in the chest? Tension in the head? An assortment of negative thoughts? Counterintuitively, bringing awareness to the sensations, mood, and thoughts while not trying to escape may lead to a decrease of the depressive state itself. Much of the suffering in a depressive state is derived from being depressed about being depressed.

Mindfulness

You've learned that mindfulness is an intentional awareness of the present moment without any judgment or criticism of that moment. This can be practiced in a discrete form such as a body scan or as a disposition brought to bear during everyday life. You can shine the spotlight of mindfulness wherever and whenever you select.

Mindfulness helps us to accept things as they are, allowing us to make skillful responses rather than merely reacting to situations. It has such power in countering depression and anxiety because it is focused on the present moment. When you focus on what is happening right now, you stop ruminating about problems in the past or worries about the future. You are able to turn down the alarm areas of your brain and enhance the problem-solving areas instead.

Mindfulness helps us view our thoughts and feelings from a decentered perspective, so that we can see these phenomena as mental events. By practicing mindfulness and decentering from depressive thoughts and feelings, you can adopt a more compassionate view of yourself. This allows you to see that thoughts are not facts, perhaps especially when you are most certain that they *are* facts.

Our thoughts about depressive states tend to amplify our distress. We expect them to continue to get worse with time, when research and experience indicate that distress levels off or actually decreases with time. This finding is consistent across virtually all physical and emotional pain states. Accepting this can reduce our suffering.

Bringing acceptance rather than self-criticism to ourselves can go a long way toward reducing our distress. For example, accepting that our mind will continue to generate anxiety-producing or depressive thoughts can paradoxically reduce our feeling compelled to pay attention to such thoughts. We can accept that our mind is not always our friend.

As we've seen, anxiety and anger can coexist with or exacerbate depression. Anxiety, involving the fear of a particular stimulus, focuses on a future catastrophe. Mindfulness, with its emphasis on the present moment, has a natural anti-anxiety effect.

The tricky thing about anger is that it can both be a potent driver of depression as well as arise from it. When you are depressed, it is common to view things negatively in ways that lead to angry interpretations. Anger often occurs when you want things to be other than the way they are, and you interpret a situation as being directed toward you personally when there is absolutely no evidence to back that up.

Compassion toward others and yourself are natural antidotes for anger. By stepping into an observing-self mode, you can bring another perspective to your situation. Applying a lens of self-compassion helps counter the shame and self-criticism so common in depression.

Keeping a mindful perspective on how you align your achievements and your expectations can be important in affecting your mood. Often in depression your sense of achievement is artificially diminished while your expectations are impossibly inflated — a recipe for feeling miserable.

Acceptance, the reciprocal of resistance, can help reduce our suffering even when the physical or emotional pain doesn't change. Acceptance and self-compassion are the two wings of equanimity that put us in a position to be even-keeled and respond skillfully to situations.

And What about MBCT?

MBCT aims at changing our *relationship* to depression without focusing on a decrease of its symptoms. In this sense, our suffering does not have to be tied to our level of symptoms. Instead of getting depressed about being depressed, we can accept it as it is and in this way be able to respond skillfully. This response could include intensifying our meditation practice but might also include seeing a therapist or psychiatrist. Sometimes the most skillful response may be to take an antidepressant medication or to adjust the dose if you are already on one. We don't have to view a new depressive episode as a personal failure, but rather as only another chapter in a long-term condition.

Think about this point. If you were an asthmatic, would you think of yourself as a failure for having an asthma episode? Or would you see it with compassion as a temporary setback to recover from? What about depression? Doesn't that deserve as much compassion?

Instead of getting depressed about being depressed, we can accept it as it is and in this way be able to respond skillfully.

MBCT is effective at preventing a relapse of your depression or residual depression. In fact, it can be as effective as maintenance medications in preventing relapse. It has been shown to be useful in a broad array of medical problems ranging from headache to cancer. Originally shown to be effective in preventing relapse, MBCT has been shown to significantly impact anxiety and depression levels while improving self-compassion and reducing rumination. These results are discussed in Appendix A.

Imaging studies indicate mindfulness meditation can have an effect on the brain patterns after eight weeks of practice. This training restores more normal patterns of emotion regulation, with activation of executive control areas such as the dorsolateral prefrontal cortex, the area of the brain in the forehead region, and decreasing alarm activations from areas such as the amygdala. These results are discussed in more detail in Appendix B.

Tips to Help You Keep Up Your Practice

I cannot recommend a specific amount of meditation for you, say, a certain number of minutes per day, that will produce a specific effect. Rather, my experience indicates that the *regularity* of practice may be more important than the length of the sessions. Remember, a mindfulness practice is just that — a practice. It is not a specific or perfectly programmed set of meditations. In fact, striving for perfection is a sure way to disappointment. This is important to remember, because depression has a tendency to distort your perception of what you are doing.

Perhaps the biggest obstacle in building your mindfulness practice is depression itself. So it is critical, when you are feeling pessimistic and having negative thoughts about your progress, to remember that those thoughts are just thoughts and not facts. Your practice will vary from one day to the next. The key is consistency of effort. Experiment with the time of day, location, position, and type of practice.

Do what works for you, whether it is shorter or longer meditations. You may be surprised at how you can fit a brief meditation into many settings. For example, a breath-counting or the three-minute meditation described at the end of this chapter may work quite nicely while on a bus or even waiting for a technical-support phone call!

I recommend that you view the various techniques in the book as a buffet of offerings and select your favorites. Use your selections to develop a practice that is right for you. Try not to be swayed by what others do. Build your portfolio of favorite meditations and use them to maintain your practice.

That said, it can be quite helpful to share your meditation practice in some way. One way is to have a meditation buddy whom you meet with on some regular basis to meditate together. You might also attend a meditation center in your area. If you do an internet search for mindfulness meditation centers in your area, you will often find quite a few to select from. Almost all are free or low-cost. You might try a few out to find one that you feel is a good fit. Realize that with the skills you've developed here, you are equipped to attend many meditation centers in your area. Some are located in Buddhist centers, because that is after all where mindfulness meditation started. But don't worry; you don't have to be Buddhist to participate in the meditation practices that are open to anyone.

If you don't live near a meditation center or a college or university where meditation groups are available, or you have other circumstances in your life that make it difficult to attend a group, another possibility is to consider using mindfulness apps. There are nearly a thousand apps offering forms of meditation. Most offer a free version or trial and then charge a modest fee for ongoing use. Some of the more popular ones include Calm, Headspace, Insight Timer, and Waking Up.

These apps typically allow you to select variables, such as length of meditation, mode (for example, guided or just timed), and type (such as body scan or sitting meditation). You can also select from among various meditation teachers or leaders. Some also allow you to join a virtual group with others or with friends. You can often see who else is meditating at the same time as you and decide to join in.

Another alternative is to find a live MBCT class. If you decide to pursue this option, I suggest that you check to see if the class is offered for relapse prevention or for active treatment of depression and anxiety. The focus of the two is somewhat different, so find out which is the best fit for your needs. Although internet searches in your area can be quite helpful, you can also check the website accessMBCT.com to find a group. It has an international directory of programs.

Finally, remember that you are welcome to use the guided meditations on the book's website, www.stuarteisendrath.com. They of course are tailored to the book and are freely available.

In closing, I want to congratulate you for having worked through this book. It takes a great deal of effort and willingness to try new approaches. I hope you have found it helpful and that it aids you in launching your mindfulness practice and a new way of relating to depression and anxiety. They won't go away, but with the help of MBCT you can learn to live with much less suffering. And that is my hope for all of us.

The following meditation, developed by Zindel Segal and colleagues,[1] takes three minutes and is usually done while sitting in a chair, but can be practiced in virtually any setting — riding on a bus, lying in bed, standing in a grocery line, or sitting at your desk. It is not aimed at distracting you from a stressful situation. Rather, it can help you focus on the present moment, letting go of ruminations and forecasting catastrophes.

TRY THIS: Three-Minute Breathing Space

Sit comfortably in a chair, close your eyes or gaze softly ahead of you, and center yourself.

First minute: First, focus on whatever physical sensations are present for you right now, such as contact points your body is making with your chair. Second, shift your focus to whatever thoughts may be present; just notice them, but do not try to debate them. Third, notice whatever feelings are present. Complete these observations without judgment.

Second minute: Narrow your focus to the breath moving in and out at the nostrils, chest, or abdomen. Keeping the focus, notice if the mind wanders and gently bring the attention back to the breath.

Third minute: Expand your awareness to the body as a whole, perhaps feeling as if your entire body is breathing (that is, expanding and contracting with each breath).

Finish by bringing your attention back to your setting in a gentle, peaceful way.

APPENDIX A

Clinical Research Results

The original research evaluating MBCT was completed by John Teasdale, Zindel Segal, and Mark Williams.[1] They developed MBCT from the platform of MBSR (Mindfulness-Based Stress Reduction). MBCT targeted the prevention of downward cognitive spirals related to depressive mood. They found that focusing attention helped people to move away from these negative spirals. They evaluated individuals who had remitted completely from an episode of depression and enrolled half of them into a course of MBCT; the other half were treated with the usual care. The MBCT group had approximately 50 percent fewer episodes of relapse over fifty-two weeks.

Following this pioneering study, the research became progressively refined. Zindel Segal and colleagues mounted a large study to compare MBCT to antidepressant treatment.[2] They found that for individuals with unstable depression (with severity scores moving in and out of remission), MBCT was as effective as antidepressant treatment.

In an even more definitive study, Willem Kuyken and colleagues evaluated individuals who had remitted with antidepressant treatment.[3] They randomized the cohort into two components. One continued to receive antidepressants for two additional years. Those in the other component were tapered off of antidepressants and given MBCT. This was a very important study, because maintenance antidepressant treatment has been considered the standard of care. They found that over the two years there was no difference in relapse rates, meaning that MBCT was just as good as maintenance antidepressants in preventing relapse.

Kuyken and colleagues also performed a meta-analysis of MBCT for the prevention of depression relapse.[4] A meta-analysis looks at overall results from a number of studies in order to base an assessment of efficacy on a larger sample. These researchers included 9 randomized clinical trials that contained 1,258 participants. They found that, compared with control groups, MBCT produced a decreased risk of depressive relapse over a yearlong follow-up period. Higher levels of depression severity before treatment were associated with greater response.

My research group completed the Practicing Alternatives to Heal from Depression (PATH-D) study.[5] This study investigated MBCT for individuals with depression who had failed to recover despite at least two antidepressant treatments. All participants were still taking an antidepressant. We compared MBCT to a control condition called the health-enhancement program, which included exercise, nutritional counseling, and music therapy and which was delivered over an eight-week period similar to that for MBCT. We found that the MBCT participants were more likely to respond, with a greater than 50 percent reduction in depression as well as an overall greater percentage reduction in depressive symptoms. MBCT participants had decreased anxiety, decreased rumination, and increased mindfulness and self-compassion. The effects persisted through the one-year follow-up of the study.

Our group also completed a pilot study of MBCT for treating individuals with active depression.[6] The individuals completed

MBCT as monotherapy, meaning they were not taking medication or in any other form of psychotherapy at the same time. We compared this group to individuals who had received a selective scrotonin reuptake inhibitor antidepressant. Although this was not a randomized trial, the two groups were matched for age, sex, and depression severity. MBCT produced similar improvements in reducing depressive symptoms. This points the way for future studies of MBCT as a potential therapeutic alternative to anti-depressants in treating depression.

Other investigators have found that MBCT has been useful in a broad variety of clinical applications. For example, researchers have studied MBCT in treating a number of conditions including insomnia, hypochondriasis, cancer, HIV disease, headache, chronic pain, attention deficit disorder, and traumatic brain injury.[7] Part of this broad utility is driven by its use on metacognitive processes such as decentering, decreased rumination, and enhanced self-compassion. All of these processes help the individual enhance emotion regulation. Even though MBCT was originally developed for depression relapse prevention, its features allow it to be a transdiagnostic treatment for a broader population.

APPENDIX B

Research Results and Brain Effects

Understanding the changes taking place in the brain in depression helps shed light on the pathological processes. If you suffer from depression, it is important to understand that depression is associated with definite brain abnormalities. In other words, there are real abnormalities, and with treatment these can be mitigated.

Although a variety of treatments are available, we now know that mindfulness interventions can help reverse brain abnormalities. Because of the brain's neuroplasticity — its ability to change and grow over time — brain circuitry and even cell density can be reshaped with mind-training techniques. Prior to the arrival of modern brain-imaging methods, it was thought that adult brains were fixed and immutable, but it is now clear that many aspects of the brain can be altered throughout adulthood.

The understanding of the pathophysiology of depression has exploded in the past decade. Instead of focusing on specific neurotransmitter activities, such as serotonin and norepinephrine, functional imaging of the brain through either functional magnetic resonance imaging (fMRI) or positron emission tomography (PET) has led to a new understanding of abnormalities in the circuitry involved in depression within the brain. The imaging is called functional, because it shows how the brain is functioning from moment to moment. It is clear that the circuitry is grossly disturbed in depressive disorders. Before describing the findings from our studies, it is useful to review some of the changes that take place in depression.

We can think of the brain as consisting of more recently developed portions, such as the cerebral cortex, and earlier developed areas, such as the limbic system. The cortex is involved in higher-level functioning such as decision making, problem solving, judgment, and emotion regulation. The limbic system, including deeper layers of the brain such as the amygdala, are more involved in processing incoming information. The limbic system filters what is salient for the cortex to process and produces alarms and calls to action. It is important to note that both higher and lower functions are not regulated solely by one specific area, but via networks of brain regions. Helen Mayberg and colleagues have developed an elaborate model of how brain functioning is altered in depression.[1] Our findings were consistent with Mayberg's model.

In our preliminary studies we utilized functional magnetic resonance imaging (fMRI) to investigate brain changes that took place with treatment. fMRI measures blood flow from second to second. This flow is considered to be a proxy for brain activity. The emotion-regulation system includes a dorsal (upper) executive control system and a ventral (lower) affective processing system. In depression, although there is some variation in studies, there is typically a decrease in the activity of the cerebral cortex, notably the left dorsolateral (above the left eye more than the right) prefrontal cortex (DLPFC) component of the dorsal executive control system. At the same time, there is increased activation of the amygdala and other circuitry in that area, such as the ventral (deeper) lateral prefrontal cortex and other areas of the ventral affective processing system of the brain.[2] These relationships are illustrated in the following graphic created by Olga Tymofiyeva, a neuroscientist at UCSF.

NORMAL MOOD

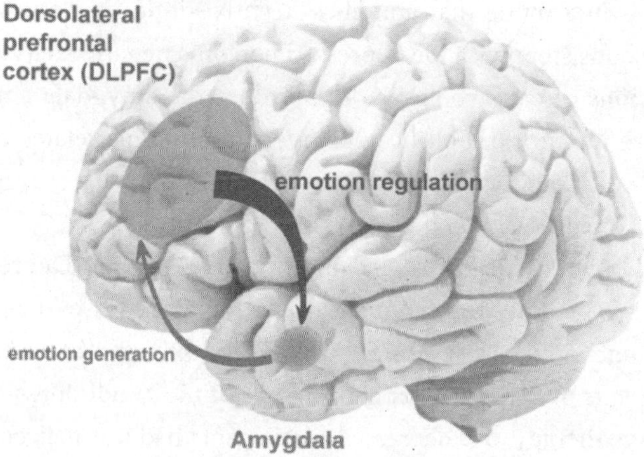

Dorsolateral prefrontal cortex (DLPFC)

emotion regulation

emotion generation

Amygdala

DEPRESSION

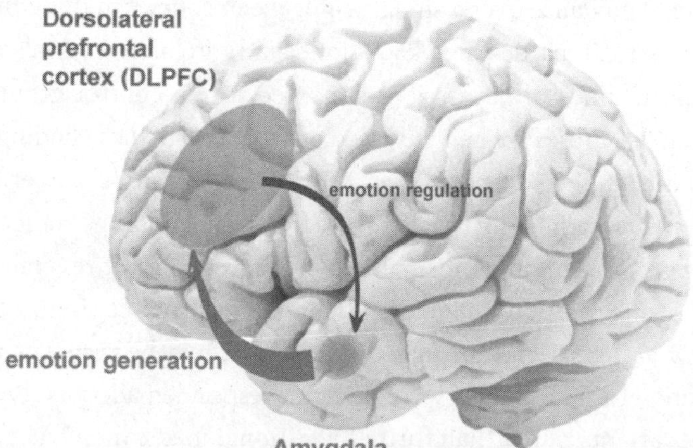

Dorsolateral prefrontal cortex (DLPFC)

emotion regulation

emotion generation

Amygdala

These findings are consistent with the clinical picture of depression. For example, if the dorsolateral prefrontal cortex is not active and functioning normally, the individual has trouble problem solving, making decisions, and recalling unbiased memories. When depressed, a person may notice the inability to think clearly or make even simple decisions. The amygdala, on the other hand, operates in a mode that amplifies negative input in depression. This is consistent with the depressed person's negative biases and predictions of catastrophe. Not only does the amygdala amplify negative input; it diminishes positive stimuli. This relates to the inability of a depressed person to recall past pleasant events, activities, or successful endeavors.

In our Practicing Alternatives to Heal from Depression (PATH-D) study, we preliminarily investigated our participants' brain functioning in several ways.[3] We looked at our depressed participants over time. After eight weeks of the mindfulness-based cognitive therapy, our depressed participants had normalized activation in the left DLPFC (it increased) and the amygdala (it decreased). This represented a reversal of the pretreatment findings. We also compared our MBCT participants to a control group of depressed participants who received exercise, music therapy, and nutritional guidance over a similar eight-week course. In this comparison, MBCT participants had significantly greater reversals of the abnormalities of depression compared to the control group.[4] Additional analyses are being carried out to validate these findings.

These findings suggest that MBCT can produce powerful brain effects with eight weeks of practice. Our findings indicate that the typical brain abnormalities of depression are reversible with this intervention. In fact, antidepressants produce similar effects. Overall these results suggest that MBCT may be a reasonable alternative for individuals who have not responded adequately to antidepressants rather than further additional medication trials.

These findings documented some of the fMRI shifts that occurred with MBCT. There has been increasing evidence that mindfulness meditation can have powerful brain effects. Richard Davidson and colleagues in 2003 found that mindfulness-based stress reduction over an eight-week course produced a shift toward activation of the left DLPFC with electrical testing.[5] Matthew Lieberman and colleagues noted that labeling emotions produced less activation of the amygdala in study participants.[6] The labeling was similar to the observing component of mindfulness. Norman Farb and colleagues found that MBSR training reduced brain pathways associated with rumination.[7] Sara Lazar, at Harvard, found that long-term meditators had increased cortical thickness in the DLPFC regions as well as increased cell mass in the insula, an area of the brain associated with awareness of bodily sensations.[8]

Britta Holzel and colleagues found that mindfulness training produced increased gray matter in specific areas of the brain.[9] These included the left hippocampus, an area associated with memory and emotion control. Gray matter was also increased in several other brain regions. These changes were associated with improvements in several measures of mindfulness. These changes did not occur in a control group.

The Practicing Alternatives to Heal from Depression (PATH-D) study was carried out in a difficult-to-treat population of individuals who had failed to recover despite two or more antidepressant trials and were currently being treated with an antidepressant. We performed a second smaller fMRI study of individuals who were off all medication and were suffering depression. The findings were the same: MBCT was associated with normalization of brain function.[10]

These studies are important because they indicate brain function can shift with "user activated" techniques. Learning mindfulness meditation can have powerful brain effects, including increasing activation of areas such as the prefrontal cortex, which is associated with enhanced emotion regulation, and down regulation of the "alarm system" in the amygdala and similar areas.

It appears that mindfulness training has effects systemically as well as in the brain. For example, in a pilot study we examined a measure of inflammation in the body for individuals completing eight weeks of MBCT.[11] We found that individuals had a significant reduction in the measure of inflammation called C-reactive protein. Similarly, J. David Creswell and colleagues in a larger study found similar results with a different measure of inflammation.[12] These findings are intriguing because there is a strong but not completely defined relationship between depression and inflammation. In some instances, evidence of inflammation precedes depression, and in others depression precedes inflammation. Although more research about the interactions of depression and inflammation are needed, it appears that mindfulness training may be an important way of probing the relationship.

ACKNOWLEDGMENTS

Many people have contributed to this book. Most important have been the many participants in the UCSF mindfulness-based cognitive therapy program at the UCSF Depression Center. I learned from all of them, and they were in-depth teachers. Some of their stories are described in the book (with their identities disguised or blended to protect privacy). I also need to thank the developers of mindfulness-based cognitive therapy, Zindel Segal, John Teasdale, and Mark Williams. All have generously shared their knowledge and wisdom. Zindel in particular has been a close teacher, supporter, and collaborator.

Meditation teachers have been illuminating along the way and are too numerous to mention in total, but include Joseph Goldstein, Jon Kabat-Zinn, Sylvia Boorstein, Sharon Salzberg, Trudy Goodman, Guy Armstrong, Jack Kornfield, and Kevin Barrows. Linda Graham's work on resilience as well as Kristin Neff's and Chris Germer's contributions to understanding the role of self-compassion have been invaluable. Steven C. Hayes has illuminated many issues through his work in acceptance and commitment therapy.

A number of people have helped in the development of our

MBCT adaptation for the treatment of depression. Foremost among these is my close collaborator Maura McLane. Without her steady hand not much would have gotten off the ground. My research team coordinator, Erin Gillung, added focused input that improved our processes tremendously. She was the glue that held our team together. Other members of the research team include Christa Hogan and Lauren Erickson, who both contributed helpful ideas. Both Maura and Erin reviewed versions of this book, adding greatly to its clarity. Maggie Chartier, Krishna Munshi, Walter Sipe, Robin Bitner, and Tracy Peng helped in the early adaptation of MBCT.

Perhaps the most essential person in bringing this book to fruition is my editor Caroline Pincus. She is appropriately known as the "book midwife" and very much played this role for me. Without her guidance, wisdom, and skills, this book would be resting on some muddy shoals. Jason Gardner, executive editor at New World Library, and copyeditor Ann Moru have also played key roles in the publishing process and deserve my most sincere thanks. Others also helped along the way with early encouragement and critiques, including Rachel Trusheim and Stan Press.

I need to thank my family, including my wife, Debra, for giving me many valuable ideas and the time for writing. Adam and Allison Eisendrath and Faina Novosolov were also supporters throughout the writing process and reviewed versions of the manuscript with numerous helpful comments.

PERMISSION ACKNOWLEDGMENTS

G rateful acknowledgment is made to the following for permission to quote from their work:

Coleman Barks, for "The Guest House," from *The Illuminated Rumi*, Maypop Books. Copyright © 1997 by Coleman Barks. All rights reserved.

Copper Canyon Press, for use of Anna Swir's "Myself and My Person," from *Talking to My Body*, translated by Czeslaw Milosz and Leonard Nathan. Port Townsend, WA: Copper Canyon Press, 1996.

Jennifer Paine Welwood, for "Unconditional," from *Poems for the Path*, self-published pamphlet, 2001.

NOTES

Foreword

1. J. Singh et al., "Intravenous Esketamine in Adult Treatment-Resistant Depression: A Double-Blind, Double-Randomization, Placebo-Controlled Study," *Biological Psychiatry* 80, no. 6 (September 15, 2016): 424–31, doi: 10.1016/j.biopsych.2015.10.018.
2. T. Anderson et al., "Microdosing Psychedelics: Personality, Mental Health, and Creativity Differences in Microdosers," *Psychopharmacology* (Berlin) 236, no. 2 (February 2019): 731–40, doi: 10.1007/s00213-018-5106-2.

Introduction

1. L. J. Cobiac and P. Scarborough, "Translating the WHO 25x25 Goals into a UK Context: The PROMISE Modelling Study," *BMJ Open* 7, no. 4 (2017): e012805; World Health Organization, *Global Burden of Disease: 2004 Update* (Geneva: World Health Organization, 2008), https://www.who.int/healthinfo/global_burden_disease/GBD_report_2004update_full.pdf.
2. T. J. Moore and D. R. Mattison, "Adult Utilization of Psychiatric Drugs and Differences by Sex, Age, and Race," *JAMA Internal Medicine* 177, no. 2 (2017): 274–75, doi: 10.1001/jamainternmed.2016.7507.
3. Z. V. Segal, J. M. Williams, and J. D. Teasdale, *Mindfulness-Based Cognitive Therapy for Depression* (New York: Guilford Press, 2002).
4. S. C. Hayes, K. Strosahl, and K. G. Wilson, *Acceptance and Commitment Therapy: The Process and Practice of Mindful Change*, 2nd ed. (New York: Guilford Press, 2012); R. D. Zettle, J. C. Rains, and S. C. Hayes, "Processes of Change in Acceptance and Commitment Therapy and Cognitive Therapy for Depression: A

Mediation Reanalysis of Zettle and Rains," *Behavior Modification* 35, no. 3 (May 2011): 265–83.

5. Segal, Williams, and Teasdale, *Mindfulness-Based Cognitive Therapy for Depression*.

6. Z. V. Segal et al., "Antidepressant Monotherapy vs. Sequential Pharmacotherapy and Mindfulness-Based Cognitive Therapy, or Placebo, for Relapse Prophylaxis in Recurrent Depression," *Archives of General Psychiatry* 67, no. 12 (2010): 1256–64; W. Kuyken et al., "Effectiveness and Cost-Effectiveness of Mindfulness-Based Cognitive Therapy Compared with Maintenance Antidepressant Treatment in the Prevention of Depressive Relapse or Recurrence (PREVENT): A Randomised Controlled Trial," *Lancet* 386, no. 9988 (2015): 63–73.

7. M. Chartier et al., "Adapting Ancient Wisdom for the Treatment of Depression: Mindfulness-Based Cognitive Therapy Group Training," *Group* (New York) 34, no. 4 (2010): 319–27; S. Eisendrath, M. Chartier, and M. McLane, "Adapting Mindfulness-Based Cognitive Therapy for Treatment-Resistant Depression: A Clinical Case Study," *Cognitive and Behavioral Practice* 18, no. 3 (2011): 362–70; S. Eisendrath et al., "A Preliminary Study: Efficacy of Mindfulness-Based Cognitive Therapy versus Sertraline as First-Line Treatments for Major Depressive Disorder," *Mindfulness* (New York) 6, no. 3 (2015): 475–82; S. J. Eisendrath et al., "A Randomized Controlled Trial of Mindfulness-Based Cognitive Therapy for Treatment-Resistant Depression," *Psychotherapy and Psychosomatics* 85, no. 2 (2016): 99–110; K. Munshi, S. Eisendrath, and K. Delucchi, "Preliminary Long-Term Follow-Up of Mindfulness-Based Cognitive Therapy–Induced Remission of Depression," *Mindfulness* (New York) 4, no. 4 (2013): 354–61.

Chapter 1. The Nature of the Depression Beast

1. K. E. James, "From Mohandas to Mahatma: The Spiritual Metamorphosis of Gandhi," *Essays in History* (Corcoran Department of History, University of Virginia), 28 (1984): 20.

2. P. J. Buckley, "Vincent van Gogh (1853–1890): Experiencing Madness," *American Journal of Psychiatry* 174, no. 7 (2017): 626–27.

3. I. C. Kaufman., "Mother-Infant Separation in Monkeys: An Experimental Model," in J. P. Scott and E. C. Senay, eds., *Separation and Depression* (Washington, DC: American Association for the Advancement of Science, 1973), 33–52.

4. A. M. Lozano et al., "A Multicenter Pilot Study of Subcallosal Cingulate Area Deep Brain Stimulation for Treatment-Resistant Depression," *Journal of Neurosurgery* 116, no. 2 (2012): 315–22; H. S. Mayberg, "Defining the Neural Circuitry of Depression: Toward a New Nosology with Therapeutic Implications," *Biological Psychiatry* 61, no. 6 (2007): 729–30.

5. A. J. Rush et al., "Bupropion-SR, Sertraline, or Venlafaxine-XR After Failure of SSRIs for Depression," *New England Journal of Medicine* 354, no. 12 (2006):

1231–42; A. J. Rush et al., "STAR*D: Revising Conventional Wisdom," *CNS Drugs* 23, no. 8 (2009): 627–47; A. J. Rush et al., "Selecting Among Second-Step Antidepressant Medication Monotherapies: Predictive Value of Clinical, Demographic, or First-Step Treatment Features," *Archives of General Psychiatry* 65, no. 8 (2008): 870–80.

6. K. Richmond, E. Zerbo, and P. Levounis, "What Is Mindfulness: A History of Mindfulness and Meditation," in E. Zerbo et al., eds., *Becoming Mindful: Integrating Mindfulness into Your Psychiatric Practice* (Arlington, VA: American Psychiatric Association Publishing, 2017), 1–8.

7. J. Kabat-Zinn, *Full Catastrophe Living: Using the Wisdom of Your Body and Mind to Face Stress, Pain, and Illness* (New York: Delacorte, 1990).

8. J. D. Benhard, J. Kristeller, and J. Kabat-Zinn, "Effectiveness of Relaxation and Visualization Techniques as an Adjunct to Phototherapy and Photochemotherapy of Psoriasis," *Journal of the American Academy of Dermatology* 19, no. 3 (1988): 572–74; J. Kabat-Zinn, L. Lipworth, and R. Burney, "The Clinical Use of Mindfulness Meditation for the Self-regulation of Chronic Pain," *Journal of Behavioral Medicine* 8, no. 2 (1985): 163–90; A. O. Massion et al., "Meditation, Melatonin and Breast/Prostate Cancer: Hypothesis and Preliminary Data," *Medical Hypotheses* 44, no. 1 (1995): 39–46; J. J. Miller, K. Fletcher, and J. Kabat-Zinn, "Three-Year Follow-Up and Clinical Implications of a Mindfulness Meditation-Based Stress Reduction Intervention in the Treatment of Anxiety Disorders," *General Hospital Psychiatry* 17, no. 3 (1995): 192–200; L. E. Carlson, "Mindfulness-Based Interventions for Coping with Cancer," *Annals of the New York Academy of Sciences* 1373, no. 1 (2016): 5–12; J. E. Owens et al., "A Randomized Controlled Trial Evaluating Mindfulness-Based Stress Reduction (MBSR) for the Treatment of Palpitations: A Pilot Study," *International Journal of Cardiology* 223 (2016): 25–27.

9. Buckley, "Vincent van Gogh."

10. V. van Gogh, *Ever Yours: The Essential Letters*, ed. L. Jansen, H. Luijten, and N. Bakker (New Haven, CT: Yale University Press, 2014), 661.

Chapter 2. What Mindfulness Is and What It Is Not

1. S. J. Eisendrath et al., "A Randomized Controlled Trial of Mindfulness-Based Cognitive Therapy for Treatment-Resistant Depression," *Psychotherapy and Psychosomatics* 85, no. 2 (2016): 99–110.

2. C. Papageorgiou and A. Wells, "Effects of Attention Training on Hypochondriasis: A Brief Case Series," *Psychological Medicine* 28, no. 1 (1998): 193–200.

3. R. M. Sapolsky, *Why Zebras Don't Get Ulcers*, 3rd ed. (New York: Holt, 2004).

4. M. A. Day and B. E. Thorn, "Mindfulness-Based Cognitive Therapy for Headache Pain: An Evaluation of the Long-Term Maintenance of Effects,"

Complementary Therapies in Medicine 33 (August 2017): 94–98, doi: 10.1016/j .ctim.2017.06.009.

5. B. Gunaratana, *Mindfulness in Plain English*, 20th anniversary ed. (Somerville, MA: Wisdom Publications, 2011), 30.

6. M. Epstein, *Thoughts Without a Thinker: Psychotherapy from a Buddhist Perspective* (New York: Basic Books, 1995).

Chapter 3. How Mindfulness Helps in Depression

1. R. Kessel et al., "Exploring the Relationship of Decentering to Health-Related Concepts and Cognitive and Metacognitive Processes in a Student Sample," *BMC Psychology* 4 (March 8, 2016): 11, doi: 10.1186/s40359-016-0115-6.

Chapter 4. Your Mind Is Not Always Your Friend

1. N. B. Schmidt, K. Jacquin, and M. J. Telch, "The Overprediction of Fear and Panic in Panic Disorder," *Behaviour Research and Therapy* 32, no. 7 (September 1994): 701–7; A. P. Wagner, "Cognitive-Behavioral Therapy for Children and Adolescents with Obsessive-Compulsive Disorder," *Brief Treatment and Crisis Intervention* 3, no. 3 (2003): 291–306.

2. D. L. Chambless and E. J. Gracely, "Fear of Fear and the Anxiety Disorder," *Cognitive Therapy and Research* 13 (1989): 9–20.

3. J. Rumi, *The Illuminated Rumi*, trans. Coleman Barks (Athens, GA: Maypop, 1997), 77.

Chapter 5. Thoughts Are Not Facts

1. E. Tolle, *The Power of Now: A Guide to Spiritual Enlightenment* (Novato, CA: New World Library, 1999), 4–5.

Chapter 6. Anxiety

1. M. M. Weissman, "Recent Advances in Depression Across the Generations," *Epidemiologia e psichiatria sociale* 15, no. 1 (2006): 16–19.

2. R. E. McMullin, *The New Handbook of Cognitive Therapy Techniques*, rev. ed. (New York: Norton, 2000), 157.

Chapter 8. Compassion and Self-Compassion

1. W. Kuyken et al., "How Does Mindfulness-Based Cognitive Therapy Work?," *Behaviour Research and Therapy* 48, no. 11 (2010): 1105–12.

2. M. Ricard, *Altruism: The Power of Compassion to Change Yourself and the World*, trans. C. Mandell and S. Gordon (New York: Little, Brown, 2015).

3. K. Neff and C. K. Germer, *The Mindful Self-Compassion Workbook: A Proven Way to Accept Yourself, Build Inner Strength, and Thrive* (New York: Guilford Press, 2018); K. Neff, *Self-Compassion: Stop Beating Yourself Up and Leave Insecurity Behind* (New York: Morrow, 2011).

4. R. Hiraoka et al., "Self-Compassion as a Prospective Predictor of PTSD Symptom Severity Among Trauma-Exposed U.S. Iraq and Afghanistan War Veterans," *Journal of Traumatic Stress* 28, no. 2 (2015): 127–33.

5. T. M. Au et al., "Compassion-Based Therapy for Trauma-Related Shame and Posttraumatic Stress: Initial Evaluation Using a Multiple Baseline Design," *Behavior Therapy* 48, no. 2 (2017): 207–21.

6. W. Kuyken et al., "How Does Mindfulness-Based Cognitive Therapy Work?," *Behaviour Research and Therapy* 48, no. 11 (2010): 1105–12.

7. Z. Gedik, "Self-Compassion and Health-Promoting Lifestyle Behaviors in College Students," *Psychology, Health & Medicine* 24, no. 1 (January 2019): 108–14, doi: 10.1080/13548506.2018.1503692.

8. A. J. Dowd and M. E. Jung, "Self-Compassion Directly and Indirectly Predicts Dietary Adherence and Quality of Life Among Adults with Celiac Disease," *Appetite* 113 (June 1, 2017); 293–300, doi: 10.1016/j.appet.2017.02.023.

9. A. Wheelis, "The Place of Action in Personality Change," *Psychiatry* 13, no. 2 (1950): 135–48.

Chapter 9. Achievements Divided by Expectations Equals Happiness

1. T. Brach, *Radical Acceptance: Embracing Your Life with the Heart of a Buddha* (New York: Bantam, 2003).

2. S. J. Eisendrath and J. Dunkel, "Psychological Issues in Intensive Care Unit Staff," *Heart & Lung: The Journal of Critical Care* 8, no. 4 (1979): 751–58; F. S. Bongard, D. Y. Sue, and J. R. E. Vintch, *Current Diagnosis & Treatment: Critical Care*, 3rd ed. (New York: McGraw-Hill Medical, 2008) 440–42.

3. J. B. Luoma, S. C. Hayes, and R. D. Walser, *Learning ACT: An Acceptance & Commitment Therapy Skills-Training Manual for Therapists* (Oakland, CA: New Harbinger, 2007), x, 304.

Chapter 10. The Difference between Pain and Suffering

1. S. Young, *The Science of Enlightenment: How Meditation Works* (Boulder, CO: Sounds True, 2016).

2. K. Ellison, "Mastering Your Own Mind," *Psychology Today*, September/October 2006, 22.

3. H. K. Beecher, "Relationship of Significance of Wound to Pain Experienced," *Journal of the American Medical Association* 161, no. 17 (1956): 1609–13.

4. C. E. Wilcox et al., "The Subjective Experience of Pain: An FMRI Study of Percept-Related Models and Functional Connectivity," *Pain Medicine* 16, no. 11 (2015): 2121–33; T. Gard et al., "Pain Attenuation Through Mindfulness Is Associated with Decreased Cognitive Control and Increased Sensory Processing in the Brain," *Cerebral Cortex* 22, no. 11 (2012): 2692–702; F. Zeidan et al., "Brain Mechanisms Supporting the Modulation of Pain by Mindfulness Meditation," *Journal of Neuroscience* 31, no. 14 (2011): 5540–48.

5. S. J. Eisendrath, "Pain, Avoidance, and Suffering," *Pain* 153, no. 6 (2012): 1134–35.

Chapter 11. Acceptance and Other Shifts in Attitude

1. R. J. Davidson et al., "Depression: Perspectives from Affective Neuroscience," *Annual Review of Psychology* 53 (2002): 545–74.

2. M. Singer, *The Untethered Soul: The Journey Beyond Yourself* (Oakland, CA; New Harbinger, 2007).

3. J. D. Creswell et al., "Neural Correlates of Dispositional Mindfulness During Affect Labeling," *Psychosomatic Medicine* 69, no. 6 (2007): 560–65.

Chapter 12. How to Live Well Despite Depression

1. Z. V. Segal, J. D. Teasdale, M. J. Williams, and M. C. Gemar, "The Mindfulness-Based Cognitive Therapy Adherence Scale: Inter-Rater Reliability, Adherence to Protocol and Treatment Distinctiveness," *Clinical Psychology and Psychotherapy* 9 (2002): 131–38.

Appendix A. Clinical Research Results

1. Z. Segal, J. M. Williams, and J. Teasdale, *Mindfulness-Based Cognitive Therapy for Depression* (New York: Guilford Press, 2002); J. D. Teasdale et al., "Prevention of Relapse/Recurrence in Major Depression by Mindfulness-Based Cognitive Therapy," *Journal of Consulting and Clinical Psychology* 68, no. 4 (2000): 615–23.

2. Z. V. Segal et al., "Antidepressant Monotherapy vs. Sequential Pharmacotherapy and Mindfulness-Based Cognitive Therapy, or Placebo, for Relapse Prophylaxis in Recurrent Depression," *Archives of General Psychiatry* 67, no. 12 (2010): 1256–64.

3. W. Kuyken et al., "Effectiveness and Cost-Effectiveness of Mindfulness-Based

Cognitive Therapy Compared with Maintenance Antidepressant Treatment in the Prevention of Depressive Relapse or Recurrence (PREVENT): A Randomised Controlled Trial," *Lancet* 386, no. 9988 (2015): 63–73.

4. W. Kuyken et al., "Efficacy of Mindfulness-Based Cognitive Therapy in Prevention of Depressive Relapse: An Individual Patient Data Meta-analysis from Randomized Trials," *JAMA Psychiatry* 73, no. 6 (2016): 565–74.

5. S. J. Eisendrath et al., "A Randomized Controlled Trial of Mindfulness-Based Cognitive Therapy for Treatment-Resistant Depression," *Psychotherapy and Psychosomatics* 85, no. 2 (2016): 99–110, doi: 10.1159/000442260.

6. S. Eisendrath et al., "A Preliminary Study: Efficacy of Mindfulness-Based Cognitive Therapy versus Sertraline as First-Line Treatments for Major Depressive Disorder," *Mindfulness* (New York) 6, no. 3 (2015): 475–82.

7. S. J. Eisendrath, ed., *Mindfulness-Based Cognitive Therapy: Innovative Applications* (Urdorf, Switzerland: Springer International, 2016).

Appendix B. Research Results and Brain Effects

1. H. S. Mayberg, "Defining the Neural Circuitry of Depression: Toward a New Nosology with Therapeutic Implications," *Biological Psychiatry* 61, no. 6 (2007): 729–30.

2. L. Wang et al., "Prefrontal Mechanisms for Executive Control over Emotional Distraction Are Altered in Major Depression," *Psychiatry Research* 163, no. 2 (2008): 143–55.

3. S. J. Eisendrath et al., "A Randomized Controlled Trial of Mindfulness-Based Cognitive Therapy for Treatment-Resistant Depression," *Psychotherapy and Psychosomatics* 85, no. 2 (2016): 99–110, doi: 10.1159/000442260.

4. S. J. Eisendrath, *Mindfulness-Based Cognitive Therapy for Depression: Clinical and Brain Effects*, 2015, https://www.youtube.com/watch?v=Uf6XMEZUrwM.

5. R. J. Davidson et al., "Alterations in Brain and Immune Function Produced by Mindfulness Meditation," *Psychosomatic Medicine* 65, no. 4 (2003): 564–70.

6. M. D. Lieberman et al., "Putting Feelings into Words: Affect Labeling Disrupts Amygdala Activity in Response to Affective Stimuli," *Psychological Science* 18, no. 5 (2007): 421–28.

7. N. A. Farb et al., "Minding One's Emotions: Mindfulness Training Alters the Neural Expression of Sadness," *Emotion* 10, no. 1 (2010): 25–33.

8. S. W. Lazar et al., "Meditation Experience Is Associated with Increased Cortical Thickness," *NeuroReport* 16, no. 17 (2005): 1893–97.

9. B. K. Holzel et al., "Mindfulness Practice Leads to Increases in Regional Brain Gray Matter Density," *Psychiatry Research* 191, no. 1 (2011): 36–43.

10. Y. Li et al., "Evaluating Metabolites in Patients with Major Depressive Disorder Who Received Mindfulness-Based Cognitive Therapy and Healthy Controls

Using Short Echo MRSI at 7 Tesla," *Journal of Magnetism and Magnetic Materials* 29, no. 3 (2016): 523–33.

11.   S. J. Eisendrath et al., "Mindfulness-Based Cognitive Therapy Associated with Decreases in C-Reactive Protein in Major Depression: A Pilot Study," *Journal of Alternative, Complementary, and Integrative Medicine* 2 (2016): 10.

12.   J. D. Creswell et al., "Alterations in Resting-State Functional Connectivity Link Mindfulness Meditation with Reduced Interleukin-6: A Randomized Controlled Trial," *Biological Psychiatry* 80, no. 1 (2016): 53–61.

INDEX

ABOUT THE AUTHOR

Stuart J. Eisendrath, MD, is professor of clinical psychiatry emeritus and researcher at the University of California, San Francisco (UCSF). He has treated a full range of depressive disorders, from mild to the most severe, over the past forty years using multiple modalities. His lectures on mindfulness-based cognitive therapy for the University of California TV (www.uctv.tv) have been viewed more than 1.5 million times. His research, funded by the National Institutes of Health, focused on clinical outcomes of depression treatments and the effects of treatments on brain recovery. One of the early adopters of MBCT, he rapidly began developing it as a modality for individuals currently in episodes of depression and has been teaching this approach for over fifteen years, including directing the mindfulness training program in the UCSF Department of Psychiatry. He was the founding director of the UCSF Depression Center as well a founding board member of the National Network of Depression Centers. He has won numerous teaching awards and is a distinguished life fellow of the American Psychiatric Association. He also has had personal experience with depression, which informs his efforts to bring MBCT to a wide audience.